IF ONLY I COULD R....... TO
THE PEOPLE I'M RELATED TO

IF
ONLY
I
COULD
RELATE
TO
THE
PEOPLE
I'M
RELATED
TO

STAN TOLER

BEACON HILL PRESS
OF KANSAS CITY

Library of Congress Cataloging-in-Publication Data

Toler, Stan.
   If only I could relate to the people I'm related to / Stan Toler.
     p. cm.
   Includes bibliographical references.
   ISBN 978-0-8341-2522-3 (pbk.)
   1. Interpersonal relations—Religious aspects—Christianity. 2. Friendship—Religious aspects—Christianity. I. Title.
   BV4597.52.T65 2010
   241'.6762—dc22

                        2010006242

To Bonnie Perry and Barry Russell—

Thanks for the confidence you have placed in me as an author. Thanks for years of great friendship and ministry through the publishing of my books. There's no other way to say it: you're simply the best!

CONTENTS

ACKNOWLEDGMENTS

It has been my delight to partner with Beacon Hill Press for more than thirty years. My first book contract came from Bud Lunn, and from that moment it has been a wonderful relationship.

Special thanks to Judi Perry, Jonathan Wright, Jerry Brecheisen, Hardy Weathers, Mark Brown, Bonnie Perry, Barry Russell, and the whole Beacon Hill team.

INTRODUCTION

꩜ Relationships are as common to life as orange traffic cones—and often as frustrating. But like traffic cones, they ultimately protect and enhance your journey. So you might as well learn your way around them. I've learned some things on my journey, so I decided to write them down. Relationships usually develop within five social networks:
- **Lifestyle**: everyday work, school, church, or community
- **Family**: immediate and extended through family relationships
- **Support**: lay or professional services
- **Development**: career contacts, referral network
- **Online**: social media network

Spiritual Relationships

My whole life and ministry have been built around relationships. Chief among them, of course, is my relationship with God. Since the day I became His child through faith in His only Son, the Lord Jesus Christ, ours has been both a *family* and *friendship* relationship. We have been in constant touch through prayer and correspondence. I've called on Him to help me spiritually, emotionally, physically, financially, and socially. And since ours is a relationship of trust, He's called on me for help once in a while. *This book offers some advice on enhancing your own relationship with God.*

Family Relationships

Second only to my relationship with God is my relationship with family—my dear wife, children, and grandchildren;

11

my parents and siblings; and my extended family members. All these are part of (I confess) my "inner circle." A songwriter proposed the question "Will the circle be unbroken?" which has been asked musically from church revivals to funeral home services to the Grand Ole Opry. The songwriter was envisioning the reunion of Christians in heaven and the hope that every family member would make it there. On earth, the circle is often broken by death or division. And yes, very human misunderstandings have tested the mettle of that circle. But for the *most* part, that circle has been my trusted source of loving affection, affirmation, inspiration, and motivation.

Anyone who isn't trying to learn about enhancing family relationships will sooner or later be as popular as a pet skunk at a picnic. My brothers say I've never had a thought I didn't write down, so rather than disappoint them in this case, I included some thoughts about enhancing your family relationships.

Friend Relationships

Friends aren't a lot different from family, except for the fact that you don't necessarily have to include them in your will. But just like family, they're around when you need them. They provide a support system of loving concern, mentoring, and shared skills.

God has given me more friends than I could ever store names in my iPhone.

- Leadership friends
- Ministry friends
- Business friends
- Sports interest friends
- Social media friends

Each of them has taught me about friendship relationships—dos and don'ts, oughts and shouldas. Yes, those "insider tips" are in this book; you'll learn friendship from the pros.

Relationship Repairs

Relationships have inherent pluses, along with a few minuses. If you've ever faced conflict, failure, or disloyalty in a relationship, then this is a must-read. I've included personal—and sometimes painful—insights from "flat tire" relationships, those with unexpected emergencies that can occur at every level of the relationship grid. You'll learn how to "change a relationship flat tire" so you can get on with your journey.

You'll learn to—

• Solve conflict

• Conquer failure

• Restore communication

• Develop loyalty

I don't know about you, but when I want advice about something I go to the veterans in the crowd—those who've "been there, done that, and bought the T-shirt." Their words are backed with a certificate of achievement that gives me confidence to act on their advice.

Relationship Champions

The Bible is a veritable hall of champions. Its anointed history highlights the lifestyles of commoner and royalty alike as they worked through relationships with their families, friends, enemies, and contenders. I've used their lives as object lessons in getting the best, even from the worst, out of human relationships. You'll learn from Christ's Sermon on the Mount outlining principles to use in your social network:

• Jonathan and David's example of friendship in the midst of political turmoil.

• Ruth and Naomi's bond that modeled the best of in-law relationships.

• Abraham and Sarah's triumph of faith over circumstances that threatened their relationship.

- Women taken in adultery who discovered real forgiveness.
- Paul and Baranabas's working relationship, which survived distrust and disloyalty.
- David's failure that resulted in an adulterous relationship, which later led to restoration.
- Hannah and Samuel's mother-son relationship, which exemplified obedience to the Lord.
- Joseph and Mary's engagement and marriage, which faced unheard-of challenges but resulted in unparalleled blessing.

Real Relationships

A rookie baseball pitcher was in a tight spot. He had just walked in two runs, the bases were loaded, there was one out, and the count was 3-0. The manager took a slow walk to the mound, patted the pitcher on the left shoulder, and took the baseball from the glove in the lefty's right hand.

"Does this mean I'm outa' the game?" the pitcher asked sadly.

The manager nodded. "Afraid so, son."

"Just like *last* time!" the frustrated rookie responded. "What am I doing wrong?"

The manager said, "Reckon it could be walking out to the pitcher's mound after they play that national anthem."

If Only I Could Relate to the People I'm Related To isn't about absolute rights and wrongs. It's about tips for improvement, about discovering *real* relationships apart from the casual or incidental. The wisdom writer said, "As iron sharpens iron, a friend sharpens a friend" (Proverbs 27:17, NLT).

As your friend, I'm excited about joining you in this discovery of getting the best out of your relationship with God, your family, your friends, and your associates.

To God be the glory.

1

RELATIONSHIPS AREN'T ENVIRONMENTALLY FRIENDLY
Real Relationships

—

))) Toys grabbed from the toy box were scattered like McDonald's bags on the median of an interstate. Oatmeal was caked like stucco on chubby cheeks, flaking off with each swipe of a little hand. The wife and mother was scrambling to make biscuits and phone calls for the surprise pitch-in dinner at the same time. And I was in my "office" reading church growth books stacked on a card table while the Sears 12-inch television set blared rhyming songs.

Such was the Toler household when our toddlers were in training to become kindergartners.

It wasn't just *any* rhyming song that held wandering attentions in that Toler training camp; they were educational sound bytes straight from a street called "Sesame." Long before computer games, our kids spent time with a television family that included, among others, a tall yellow bird, a friendly red monster, and a grouchy purple monster who lived in a government-subsidized garbage can. They were part of the foam-filled cast on

15

Sesame Street who created little pre-customers who memorized cereal commercials and asked for hand puppets at Christmas.

Nearby in the same television subdivision lived the *Muppets* family, complete with a pig who wore makeup and a frog named Kermit who also had a singing career and a hit song titled "Bein' Green."

Kermit's lament that it's not easy being green is still true. And as those who are caretakers know, taking care of planets and people can be daunting tasks. For example, in an ever-moving world, relationships with people are sometimes as permanent as ice cubes in a glass of sweet tea in the Mojave Desert.

Why Isn't There a "U" in Relationship?

I think there's an even greater difference between friendships, acquaintances, and affiliations—and a "real relationship." Let me define it this way: a "real relationship" is a next-level friendship or partnership between two people who focus on mutual understanding, respect, and support in order to accomplish a mutually creative, common good. There really should be a "u" in "relationship."

"Real relationship" is a next-level friendship or
partnership between two people who focus
on mutual understanding, respect, and support
in order to accomplish a mutually creative,
common good.

Olympic champion and fellow West Virginian Mary Lou Retton compared relationships to the pattern of a quilt: "The relationships we share with people in our lives are a bit like the squares of cloth that make up a quilt—as completely different, or even opposite, as they may be, they all have a unique purpose and value that contribute to the larger pattern of our lives."[1]

16

How do we take relationships to the next level? Though the very word "relationship" suggests relating to another person, I guess Mr. Webster added a "ship" to "relation" just to let us know there would be a journey involved. Building relationships will take your best efforts—and then some.

I heard the story of a man who saw himself as God's answer to every question. Well, at least he made an *attempt* at answering every question—even before he was asked! Being an entrepreneur and experiencing some of the stuff that goes with success, he was never too shy either to display it or to talk about it.

One of his associates soon bought the hype. *If "location, location, location" is the secret to real estate,* the associate thought, *I had better get to know this entrepreneur better.* Soon he had a plan: he would take the guy out to the fanciest restaurant in town and buy him a steak so thick he would have to use a chain saw to cut it.

The restaurant night arrived, and the plan was put in motion. Sure enough, the entrepreneur was impressed by the budding buddy's attempt to win his favor. About dessert time, the associate got up the nerve to suggest that they meet again for another round of steak-eating and conversation.

"In fact," the associate said, "I think we could become pretty good friends."

The entrepreneur sank his ship in a hurry, "Well, I'll have to think about it. I'm not really looking for any particular friend right now."

The associate was startled and a bit humiliated but made a classic comeback, "Oh—well, that's okay. As you can see from my being here, I'm not exactly known for being particular."

It's in the Book

Fortunately, the book on relationships has already been written. And fortunately, someone has followed the instructions with such finesse that billions of people want to build their own relationships just like Him—Jesus of Nazareth. He was the fulfillment of the ancient promise of "a friend who sticks closer than a brother" (Proverbs 18:24).

Born on the wrong side of town, Jesus had an influence so great that no earthly metropolis could hold His followers. He had to build them a place beyond the stars, as wide as the heavens, in order to get them all in.

What Jesus the Christ says about living in general He also says about building relationships in particular in the greatest sermon ever preached: the Sermon on the Mount (see Matthew 5—7.)

No bestselling author of modern time could say anything more relevant than what has already been said about one person's relation to another.

I read of a new bride who complained to her new hubby that she had been expecting an old-fashioned marriage. Tearfully she said, "Harold, I don't see anything old-fashioned about our marriage. Why, it's been thirty-six hours since you said, 'I love you.'"

"Has not," her computer-literate husband replied. "I wrote it on your Facebook wall just last night."

No, relationships aren't always easy. Relational drought and earthquakes and hurricanes and floods of neglect are just some of the hazards people encounter in friendships, marriages, and educational or business environments. That's why the principles of God's Word are so vital in working with others to meet our personal goals.

Pleading the Fifth

From the fifth chapter of Matthew through the seventh, Jesus preached the greatest sermon over heard. It was like an owner's manual for His creation—including a parts list.

Jesus taught in Matthew 5:38-48,

You have heard that it was said, "Eye for eye, and tooth for tooth." But I tell you, Do not resist an evil person. If someone strikes you on the right cheek, turn to him the other also. And if someone wants to sue you and take your tunic, let him have your cloak as well. If someone forces you to go one mile, go with him two miles. Give to the one who asks you, and do not turn away from the one who wants to borrow from you. You have heard that it was said, "Love your neighbor and hate your enemy." But I tell you: Love your enemies and pray for those who persecute you, that you may be sons of your Father in heaven. He causes his sun to rise on the evil and the good, and sends rain on the righteous and the unrighteous. If you love those who love you, what reward will you get? Are not even the tax collectors doing that? And if you greet only your brothers, what are you doing more than others? Do not even pagans do that? Be perfect, therefore, as your heavenly Father is perfect.

I can almost hear you gasp when you read the word "perfect." Perfection and relationships seem to be an implausible combination. One ol' boy said he heard of a married couple celebrating their 50th anniversary who said they hadn't heard a cross word from each other in all those years. "Of course not," his friend replied, "They're so frugal, they haven't bought batteries for their hearing aids in the last 10 years at least!"

We can pursue the goal in the power of the Holy Spirit.

Here's the deal—only someone who is perfect can empower another to perform to perfection. The apostle Paul said of Christ, "We proclaim him, admonishing and teaching everyone with all wisdom, so that we may present everyone perfect in Christ (Colossians 1:28). Note the words "in Christ." Human perfection—including perfect relationships—is not possible. *Heavenly* perfection is! We can pursue the goal in the power of the Holy Spirit by living a Spirit-filled life.

Heaven's resource is the fuel that makes the machinery of human relationships run—perfectly.

We live by faith in the power of God's Holy Spirit to accomplish His purpose on earth through us—including building relationships with others. His perfect love can fill us and flow through us in such a way that our best qualities help to form the foundation for that relationship.

So aim for the best in God's love and strength. Do all you can do and be all you can be to make your relationship with others the best it can be. How? The clues are in the Sermon on the Mount.

1. Treat others as if their survival depended on you. "Give to the one who asks you, and do not turn away from the one who wants to borrow from you" (Matthew 5:42).

A restaurant in my hometown of Oklahoma City was the scene of a great reunion a while back. Two gentlemen in their mid-eighties shared a hug and then sat down to reminisce about the first time they met, sixty-five years earlier, at an army hospital in England during World War II. They had been wounded in the D-Day landings. Hall Duncan and my friend W. M. Lynch shared war stories and fond memories that only they could understand—like Lynch writing letters for Duncan, whose writing hand had been injured by a sniper's bullet.

Dr. Lynch, a retired Church of the Nazarene district superintendent, said, "There's something special about a relationship with the guys you lived through a very difficult time with." A weathered name and address on the back cover of a pocket-sized journal and the marvels of computer technology had brought them together. Duncan said, "We really were dependent on one another to pull through."[2]

⟪◆⟫⟪◆⟫⟪◆⟫

Relationships are planted and cultivated by unselfish personal concern.

Relationships don't grow spontaneously, as weeds do. Relationships are planted and cultivated by unselfish concern, as a beautiful rose is. They're based on the premise that one person's needs—emotional, physical, financial, or spiritual—are fulfilled through the words and actions of another. Withdrawing or withholding those factors will result in the weakening of the relationship and jeopardizing the personal welfare of the second party.

This is seen in God's relationship with us: "The LORD God is a sun and shield; the LORD bestows favor and honor; no good thing does he withhold from those whose walk is blameless" (Psalm 84:11).

In my book *I Love God's Sense of Humor; I Just Wish He'd Let Me in on the Joke* I tell of three guys stranded on an island. A bottle drifts to shore, and when they pop open the top of the bottle, a genie appears to grant the celebrated three wishes, each man receiving a single wish. The first man wishes to be reunited with his family. *Poof!* The man vanishes from the island. The second man wishes to return to his hometown. He, too, suddenly disappears, leaving one wish and one person remaining.

The genie presses for a wish from the lone survivor. After some deep thought, the third man says, "Oh, all right. I wish those two guys were back here."[3]

In real relationships, you treat others as if their personal survival depended on you. That treatment may include—
- Complimenting their strengths
- Recognizing their efforts
- Supporting their spiritual life with prayer and fellowship
- Serving as their mentor or counselor
- Lending them a financial hand when needed

- Assisting them without being asked
- Forgiving their faults.

How about it? What can you do to help someone survive his or her circumstances?

Author Stephen Covey wrote, "The most important ingredient we put into any relationship is not what we say or what we do, but what we are."[4]

2. Strive to take in those whom others leave out. "Love your enemies and pray for those who persecute you" (Matthew 5:44).

Not everyone is *always* on his or her best behavior. That doesn't mean *you* can't be, however. You have a choice in the matter. You can be a real-life example of faith under fire. Honored football coach Tony Dungy said he learned from his father that a soft answer was more effective than harsh words. His championship coaching record proves the point. In his best-selling book *Quiet Strength* Tony illustrates it in recounting his words to players at a team meeting in Tampa:

I don't yell a lot. In fact, yelling will be rare. When I get mad . . . I usually talk at the same volume I'm talking now. And when I get really mad . . . I whisper. So if my voice at this level won't get your attention, and you believe you need someone to yell at you to correct you or motivate you, then we'll probably need to find you another team to play for so that you can play your best.[5]

I don't know if the psalmist knew anything about football, but this advice in Psalm 13 will play in any stadium: "My enemy will say, 'I have overcome him,' and my foes will rejoice when I fall. But I trust in your unfailing love; my heart rejoices in your salvation" (Psalm 13:4-5). You don't have to have the last word. Trust God to have it. Not only is His grace sufficient for your *salvation*—it's also sufficient for your *conversation*.

A short breath and a prayer before speaking in a tense relational moment will give you enough time to gather your thoughts and put them through the filter of grace. God's whispers to others will be louder than your loudest shout!

3. Make it all about others. "When you give to the needy, do not announce it with trumpets, as the hypocrites do in the synagogues and on the streets, to be honored by men" (Matthew 6:2).

Christian humorist and YouTube phenom Anita Renfroe was asked in a *Reader's Digest* interview what advice she had received from her mother. She replied, "When I was a self-conscious teen, she told me, 'You think people are thinking about your zit or your large nose, but they're not. No one else is thinking of you as much as you think they are, because just think how much you're not thinking of other people.'"[6]

The greatness of a person is in his or her compassion toward others.

Some of the highest-profile people I've known never acted as if they were thinking about themselves. Whenever I would meet with them, I would walk away feeling better about myself rather than being impressed by their fame or achievement. They had the skill of making it all about others. This has been an important life lesson. The greatness of a person is in his or her compassion toward others.

Jesus exemplified it in His meeting with Zacchaeus, a wealthy man from Jericho who was curious about the Galilean. Because of the crowds following Jesus and the fact that from all that's been written about him, he might have been just slightly taller than a penguin, Zacchaeus climbed a tree for a better look.

When Jesus reached the spot, he looked up and said to him, "Zacchaeus, come down immediately. I must stay at your house today." So he came down at once and welcomed him gladly. All the people saw this and began to mutter,

"He has gone to be the guest of a 'sinner.'" But Zacchaeus stood up and said to the Lord, "Look, Lord! Here and now I give half of my possessions to the poor, and if I have cheated anybody out of anything, I will pay back four times the amount." Jesus said to him, "Today salvation has come to this house, because this man, too, is a son of Abraham. For the Son of Man came to seek and to save what was lost" (*Luke 19:1-10*).

Compare the Christ in that meeting to the red-carpet preening of many of today's personalities. Most of them act as if they're champion poodles in a hamster show. Jesus had created the tree limb that Zacchaeus was perched on, but His *heavenly majesty* was not more important to Him than His *earthly mission*.

What is your mission—or should I say, *Who* is your mission?

4. Remember: people are worth more than things. "Do not store up for yourselves treasures on earth, where moth and rust destroy, and where thieves break in and steal. But store up for yourselves treasures in heaven, where moth and rust do not destroy, and where thieves do not break in and steal (Matthew 6:19-20).

It's almost sundown. A thousand people had asked a thousand or more questions. The Master had answered all of them with a story or an object lesson. Now a successful leader, Nicodemus asks for a private meeting (see John 3). There were no "handlers" there to make up some puny excuse why Jesus couldn't meet with him that evening.

Jesus set the agenda, which had been handed to Him the day He left heaven. One person had a spiritual question that could be asked only in the swift shadows of sundown. That was enough. Jesus spent His life on earth investing in people. And now that He has ascended into heaven, He's praying for their spiritual success.

Though He attended worship and teaching services in the synagogues and the Temple, it doesn't appear He spent any time on the church board or the building committee. He was a people-builder, not a building-builder. The Bible says, "Jesus went throughout Galilee, teaching in their synagogues, preaching the good news of the kingdom, and healing every disease and sickness among the people" (Matthew 4:23). He spent His time with people—

- pouring the foundations of trust,
- fortifying the walls of security,
- installing the windows of truth,
- raising the ceilings of hope.

Now obviously I'm not against building programs or leadership by committee. I've been involved with numerous building projects and have taught church leadership in seminars and conferences around the world. But the majority of my time has been spent on building relationships with people, whether standing alongside them at a sporting event, sharing a cup of coffee at a local restaurant, praying with them at the bedside of a dying loved one, celebrating with them at their wedding, or leading them into a personal faith in Christ.

The relationships that have been forged in life are my greatest treasure.

People are worth more than things. A solid friendship has intrinsic value that won't be seen on a stock market ticker; yet it's worth more than gold.

Put people first.

5. Be on the defense team, not the jury. "In the same way you judge others, you will be judged, and with the measure you use, it will be measured to you" (Matthew 7:2).

Two golfers, one the club pro and the other his student, were on the ninth hole of the course. The only reason the pro was golfing with the student was because he was the nephew of the course's owner and had demanded it. The pro had been trying to teach the student not to raise his head when he took a swing—but to no avail.

The ninth hole was the toughest on the course, especially this day. The greens were playing as if they had been greased with lard, the roughs were so tall it took an all-terrain vehicle just to get to a lost ball, and the sand traps were so large there were camels grazing in them.

A hundred yards from the tee was a water hazard that looked to be the size of Lake Michigan. "You go first," the club pro said to the know-it-all nephew.

The student stepped to the tee, looked at the water, took a practice swing, looked at the water, adjusted the tee, and then looked at the water again. Finally he went back to the cart, put his driver into the golf bag, turned around, and started walking toward the water.

"What are you doing?" the club pro yelled.

The student golfer yelled back, "All my life I've wanted to be a profession golfer! I'll never be a professional golfer! I'm going to jump into that water and end it all!"

The club pro yelled, "No—you won't end it all! You can't keep your head down long enough!"

Everyone can be a friend, but it takes focused determination to be a friend to the *end*. In a courtroom situation the defense attorney and his or her team are those who believe in the innocence of the defendant until the very end—and sometimes beyond. There's always that shred of innocence that keeps hope alive for the defense team.

Not every condemnation is based on fact. Not every witness is plausible. There's usually one redeeming quality in the defendant's life that gives the defense team a ray of faith in the human race.

Granted, some proven crimes and sentenced criminals seem to have crossed the line, and some acts are indefensible.

But someone in the courtroom believes in the criminal no matter how despicable the accusation.

I heard of a man whose defense attorney was trying to convince the judge that her client had at least one redeemable quality. The judge was about to sentence him to serve time in Uncle Sam's Bed and Breakfast. "Your Honor," the attorney began to plead, "everything you've heard about my client has been *negative, negative, negative*. Let me remind you that he does have redemptive qualities."

The judge replied, "And what might those be?"

The defense attorney moved closer to the bench and held out one of the exhibits that had been used in the trial. "Your Honor, this sticky note he handed to the bank teller was written on recycled paper!"

Real relationships are redemptive.

Real relationships are redemptive. The same Jesus who asked His followers not to judge others became an innocent victim of the crowd's accusations and hung between common criminals on a cross. His final plea on His own behalf: "Father, forgive them."

6. Turn your vulnerability into strength. "How can you say to your brother, 'Let me take the speck out of your eye,' when all the time there is a plank in your own eye?" (Matthew 7:4).

What do you bring to a relationship? You might say, "Not much. I can't even pass a mirror without looking to see if my hair is combed!"

Humans behave in human ways. No matter how much you accomplish in your life, you know how vulnerable you are deep inside. But that knowledge isn't a weakness; rather it's strength. The apostle Paul said of his relationship with God in light of his own weaknesses,

To keep me from becoming conceited because of these surpassingly great revelations, there was given me a thorn in my flesh, a messenger of Satan, to torment me. Three times I pleaded with the Lord to take it away from me. But he said to me, "My grace is sufficient for you, for my power is made perfect in weakness." Therefore I will boast all the more gladly about my weaknesses, so that Christ's power may rest on me. That is why, for Christ's sake, I delight in weaknesses, in insults, in hardships, in persecutions, in difficulties. For when I am weak, then I am strong (*2 Corinthians 12:7-10*).

**Your vulnerability to another person
is a necessary quality.**

Real relationships are built on mutual support. Your vulnerability to another person is a necessary quality. If you were superhuman, you wouldn't need the strengths that another person can provide.

I've learned some lessons in being human:

- Asking for assistance shows your confidence in another person.
- Admitting you don't know an answer gives another person opportunity to share his or her knowledge.
- Confessing that you were wrong gives another person the right to admit his or her own failures.
- Sharing some of your own fears gives another person room to be afraid and not be ashamed.

I've never enjoyed long vacations, because the longer I'm away, the more I think about what needs to be done back home. Several years ago I learned to take mini-vacations. I've found they relax me more than long trips. A while back I called my roommate from college days, and we reminisced about some of those serious and silly moments that go along with spending four years basically with the same people. By the end of the conversation, we decided on a mini-reunion in New York City.

Several weekends later, my wife and I joined my friend and his wife in the city that never sleeps—and I'll admit none of our foursome got that much rest either. It was a whirlwind of memories, jokes, shopping, eating out, late-night talk sessions, and taking in a Broadway play. When we were getting ready to leave, my buddy from college days said, "Stan, you know, old friends are the best friends." What did he mean?

- He meant that both of us knew we had invested in each other's lives.
- He meant that we had survived normal disagreements and overlooked human faults, that we had learned the give-and-take that goes into a long-lasting relationship.
- He meant that, looking back, we saw that we had practiced those things that had turned a friendship into a "real relationship."

2

I DON'T NEED ENEMIES-
I HAVE FRIENDS I CAN'T
GET ALONG WITH
Real Friendship

Like a tree, friendship is a relationship that has blossomed with care. It has been given the right amount of light, nourishment, weeding, and soil. An *acquaintanceship* can be as casual as a conversation about health insurance at a convenience store. Friendship is a stronger tie that develops through social networks; and *real* friendship is of the next-level quality.

Relationships usually develop within five social networks:
- **Lifestyle**—everyday work, school, church, or community
- **Family**—extended through family relationships
- **Support**—lay or professional services
- **Development**—career contacts, referral network
- **Online**—social media network

A travel agent excitedly opened the envelope handed to her by the boss during a sales meeting. She shouted with joy as she read the note inside: "Congratulations! You have just won a trip to Montego Bay!"

As soon as she got home, she began to Google "Montego Bay," to make sure she saw all the sites she could during her stay. After searching a chamber of commerce web site, she made sure to visit a tourist area known for its zip line (rope slide) through a rain forest and across a scenic river.

When she got to Montego Bay, her first trip was to the zip line. As she harnessed up for the wild ride, she glanced at the deep ravine she was about to cross, then noticed that a piece of rope attached to her safety harness looked a bit frayed. "How often do you replace these ropes?" she asked.

The attendant continued to hook the travel agent into the safety harness and replied, "Whenever they break."

Sometimes the cords of friendship within your social network may be frayed by circumstances, misunderstandings, or "third-party assistance." You'll have the immediate task of strengthening the cords.

In spite of the risks, being in a firm friendship with members of your social networks is better than the alternative. I love to see people bind themselves to each other as kindred spirits, each seeking the good of the other while working toward a common goal.

Real friendship closes the gaps in our lives and makes us stronger. The devotion of a friend is an underserved and immeasurable gift.

Friends are friends through *sick and slim*.

Friendship relationships within our social network are often forged on the anvil of shared adversity. The Bible portrays such relationship in a vivid way. Interwoven through the story of Israel's King Saul and his murderous plot to destroy David, the young soldier who destroyed the enemy Philistines' Goliath, is the account of the extraordinary friendship between David and Jonathan. Saul's son Jonathan was David's closest friend.

Let's face it: you really do need friends. That's why it's important to look for friendship *templates*—real-life examples of real friendships that can be modeled in your own life. Some of those qualities can be seen in the friendship between Jonathan and David.

Theirs was a friendship that survived the thick fires of kingdom politics and slim promises. As Saul looked back on David's celebrated victory against Goliath—the Philistine's super-warrior—with five smooth stones and a sling, it soon became a source of envy for the king. He saw reality-show-super-star potential in David and was threatened by it. So he made a vow to vote him off the stage. Jonathan befriended him.

From that day Saul kept David with him and did not let him return to his father's house. And Jonathan made a covenant with David because he loved him as himself. Jonathan took off the robe he was wearing and gave it to David, along with his tunic, and even his sword, his bow and his belt (*1 Samuel 18:2-4*).

The bond of these two men—one born to pastures, one to palaces—shows us how friendships can rise above social positioning and ideological differences.

Some revisionists have tried to cheapen their relationship, suggesting that it was an immoral one. I don't believe it. God's Word is as holy as it is true. God would not excuse immorality by using it in a positive illustrative way. The relationship of Jonathan and David was both platonic and pure. They were true friends. In fact, covenants of life-long brotherhood were common in biblical times.

But their brotherhood-friendship may have an even deeper significance. It surely could have been an example of the unity of the Spirit that would be seen in the lives of New Testament believers who shared a common faith in Christ: "In Christ we who are many form one body, and each member belongs to all the others" (Romans 12:5).

The prophet Samuel tells of the constant struggle that divided David from Saul and of the running attempts to extinguish the perceived threat to Saul's reign. Saul's son Jonathan took notice of the humble courage of David in the light of those threats and became his friend—putting his own life on the line as a result.

Together, they were like survivors on a battlefield, each depending on the other for emotional strength and stability. "After David had finished talking with Saul, Jonathan became one in spirit with David, and he loved him as himself" (1 Samuel 18:1).

Friendship Factor

Alan Loy McGinnis offered criteria for friendship in what he calls the "friendship factor," which you may use as a checklist:

- Do you have at least one person nearby on whom you can call in times of personal distress?
- Do you have several people whom you can visit with little advance warning without apology?
- Do you have several people with whom you can share recreational activities?
- Do you have people who will lend you money if you need it or who will care for you in practical ways if the need arises?[1]

Friendship is a factor in physical health. According to a New York Times report, "A 10-year Australian study found that older people with a large circle of friends were 22 percent less likely to die during the study period than those with fewer friends. A large 2007 study showed an increase of nearly 60 percent in the risk for obesity among people whose friends gained weight. And last year, Harvard researchers reported that strong social ties could promote brain health as we age."[2]

Friendship is a factor in spiritual health. There are some surprising statistics about the power of friendship—especially in the context of the Church. A Gallup study commissioned by Group Publishing shows that people with close friendships in their church are—

- Very satisfied with their congregation;
- Less likely to leave their place of worship;
- Have a strong friendship with God.
- Church members who have a best friend at church are twenty-one-percent more likely to report attending at least once a week and twenty-six-percent more likely to report having a strong, more active faith in God.[3]

Friendship is a factor in vocational success. The benefits of turning acquaintances into friends within your social network far outweigh the negatives. I believe that friendships promote better productivity, among other things. For example, the worker who knows that his or her supervisor is a friend as well as an overseer will work more diligently and with greater respect.

Les and Leslie Parrot wrote,

Friends make the ordinary—running errands or eating lunch, for example—extraordinarily fun. And good friends ease our pain and lighten our heavy loads. . . . Friends help us ward off depression, boost our immune system, lower our cholesterol, increase the odds of surviving with coronary disease, and keep stress hormones in check. A half dozen top medical studies now bear this out. What's more, research is showing that you can extend your life expectancy by having the right kind of friends.[4]

Friendship Grid

If you would grid some common principles that turn acquaintanceships into friendships, they would surely be seen in the friendship of Jonathan and David.

1. They were reliable. David knew he could depend on Jonathan. Almost everyone else around him had ulterior mo-

34

R-E-A-L Friendship			
Reliable	**Ethical**	**Available**	**Loyal**
• Punctual • Thoughtful • Not afraid to laugh • There in time of need • Credible	• Keep word • Speaks honestly • Keeps confidences • Trustworthy • Kind	• Communicates • Listens • Flexible • Reciprocates • Teachable • Understanding	• Faithful in good or bad times • Defends reputations • Avoids negative talk • Non-judgmental • Affirming

tives that didn't include his welfare. Reliability is a key factor in building real relationships. I don't mean the kind of reliability that is calendar or clock oriented—though tardiness or forgetfulness can have negative effects on a friendship. I'm talking about core reliability, reliability that pledges the strength and spirit of one to the other.

Jonathan said to David, "Go in peace, for we have sworn friendship with each other in the name of the LORD, saying, 'The LORD is witness between you and me, and between your descendants and my descendants forever'" (*1 Samuel 20:42*).

I read of a man who approached the pharmacist at a corner drugstore. "How may I help you today?" the friendly pharmacist asked. The customer replied, "I need something for hiccups. Do you have something that's reliable and quick?"

The pharmacist said, "Yes, of course. Turn around and face the parking lot." The man was puzzled, but he was desperate for a remedy, so he followed the instructions. Stepping back from the counter, he turned around. The pharmacist quietly and quickly came around the corner at the other end of the counter, sneaked up behind the man, and shouted into his ear, "Boo!"

The customer nearly jumped off the floor and began to shake like a willow in a wind tunnel. "There," the pharmacist said. "Did that help?"

The customer regained his composure and nervously replied, "Not that much. My wife is the one with hiccups, and she's sitting out there in the car!"

In one sense, reliability is its own remedy. Reliability is like the grout that holds wall tile together; it's more about solidity than show.

What characterizes someone as being reliable? I think this is a pretty good checklist:

- **Punctual**—Do you try to keep your appointments? Are you on time?
- **Thoughtful**—Do you remember the little things—thank-yous, birthdays, holidays, promotions, births, deaths?
- **Not afraid to laugh**—Do you have a positive sense of humor (laugh *with*, not *at*)? Can you see the lighter side of the situation?
- **There in time of need**—Do you purposefully stand with someone during bad times?
- **Credible**—Do you strive to keep your friendships open and honest?

Are you reliable? Can your social network really depend on you? If everyone else around them seems to be against them, will you be known as the one who will be there? Late columnist Walter Winchell once said, "A real friend is one who walks in when the rest of the world walks out."[5]

2. They were ethical. David was breathless from fear and from running and looking over his shoulder, waiting for the first sight of an enemy soldier. They met at the agreed-upon time in the rocky and cold crags overlooking the city. David's first words were panic-filled yet pure: "What have I done? What is my crime? How have I wronged your father that he is trying to take my life?" (1 Samuel 20:1).

Jonathan may have rested his hand on the shoulder of David as he reassured his friend: "You are not going to die! Look, my father doesn't do anything, great or small, without confiding in me" (1 Samuel 20:2). Both had character as strong as their bond.

The ethics meter has had its ups and downs in our current culture.

I read the story of a third-grader who was asked to tell his class about his family. The teacher said, "Scotty, tell the class what your father does."

Scotty addressed the class. "Well, weekdays my father is a firefighter, but on the weekends he plays drums for a heavy metal rock band."

Envious oohs and aahs echoed off the walls of the classroom.

At the end of the school day, the teacher called Scotty to her desk. "Scotty, why did you tell the class your father was a firefighter and a drummer in a rock band? I know your father, and I know he works as an auditor for the government."

Scotty replied, "Miss Gilroy, if *your* father kept the books for *this* government, would *you* have told 'em?"

It was a pointed question. Unethical practices have a trickle-down effect. But you don't have to be a part of the new normal; you can make a difference that will bring healing and wholeness to your real friendships. An ethical friend—

- **Keeps his or her word**—"You have my word on it!" That should be more than a slogan—it should be a character quality. A friendship heads south faster than raindrops in a monsoon when a friend's word isn't dependable.
- **Speaks honestly**—"Trust me." A real friend is willing to give a life-changing opinion. Without being pushy, he or she will provide the balance between the bows and the "boos" of life. You've heard someone advise another about not approaching a certain subject: "Trust me—you don't want to go there." Real friends are real advisors.
- **Keeps confidences**—"I can keep a secret." There are times when those five words have resulted in a career car

wreck—someone who thought he or she could *couldn't*. Something said in secret suddenly shows up in an e-mail or on a cell phone call. Walter Winchell said, "I usually get my stuff from people who promised somebody else that they would keep it a secret."[6] Trace the fault lines in a fractured relationship, and they'll often go back to the moment when someone's word was broken.

- **Trustworthy**—"You can count on me." We all have a friend like that. The best of the best is wrapped in his or her integrity, inspiration, and holy influence. Someone needs you to be a best friend—best in every sense of the word.

- **Kind**—"Let me know if I can help." Mother Teresa said, "Kind words can be short and easy to speak, but their echoes are truly endless."[7] There are situations when deeds are either awkward or unnecessary, but a kind word always works. Out-of-the-blue, from-the-heart, and unexpected comments are the cure for the "common *cold*" (<http://www.brainyquote.com/quotes/quotes/m/mothertere130839.html>).

3. They were available. We don't have the advantage of seeing Jonathan's and David's Outlook calendars on their PCs or the appointment apps on their iPhones, but you can be sure they were friends who could be trusted 24/7/365—and 366 in a leap year. I have friends I can call at *any time* of the day or night. They will pray with me, counsel me, correct me, or just give me a potent dose of humor—the medicine of life. Those same friends know they can call *me* at any time as well. Availability is a strong character quality of real friendship.

Have you effectively communicated to your social network that you're available?

- **Do you communicate?** Do you stay in touch with them? Do they know from your text message, tweets, Facebook writes, notes, or e-mails that you're available?

- **Do you listen?** When you're with them, whose concern is paramount? Do you choose to make your conversations all about them instead of all about you?
- **Are you flexible?** Are you willing to drop what you're doing to take their phone calls? Do you make necessary adjustments in your calendar to meet with them?
- **Are you reciprocal?** Friendships aren't all about giving; sometimes they're about receiving, accepting a friend's help or support. In those times, when friends do you a favor, do you return the favor in like manner? There's a common adage these days that says, "Be kind to your children—they'll be making decisions about your nursing home." Jesus' principle in Luke 6:38 is a word to the wise: "Give, and you will receive. Your gift will return to you in full measure, pressed down, shaken together to make room for more, and running over" (NLT). The amount you give will determine the amount you get back.
- **Are you teachable?** Who wants to be known as the "ask. com" in a friendship? Does your friend simply submit questions because you'll always have answers, or are you willing to learn from another?
- **Are you understanding?** "I'm sorry, but I can't keep our golf date this week." How do you respond? Do you make your friend feel as if he or she just chopped down a Sequoia tree in front of a crowd of extreme environmentalist? Or do you convey an understanding attitude?

Friendships may just happen—two people may just hit it off—but friendships won't be lengthened or strengthened without a little bit of social elbow grease.

I saw the look in the driver's eyes. It was a mix of pride and anxiety. He had just committed a hit-and-run, mortally wounding a rubber orange cone left by the highway crew. There it lay, dented and forsaken by the side of the road, in the wake of a driver who had already maneuvered a legion of its brothers on his way home from Wal-Mart. Had he only remembered that cone zones in summer are as common as potholes in spring!

When the United States government offered a financial boost to the stumbling economy in 2009, it proposed putting people to work on road construction projects. Stimulating the economy resulted in hiring temporary workers for constructing or reconstructing bad roads. As a result, cone zones blossomed across many areas of the country like dandelions in spring—and often met with the same enthusiasm. Drawing the analogy, *real* friendship is always a "cone zone," a work in progress with the ever-present possibility of a real blossoming.

Be available. Of course we've built some tech barriers into our culture—answering machine messages, caller ID, cell phone alerts—but we can be the ones to tear down the barriers with some old-fashioned availability.

4. They were loyal. It was significant that Jonathan sealed his covenant of brotherhood with David by giving him his cloak. "Jonathan took off the robe he was wearing and gave it to David, along with his tunic, and even his sword, his bow and his belt" (1 Samuel 18:4).

Bible commentators Jameison, Faucett, and Brown wrote, "To receive any part of the dress which had been worn by a sovereign, or his eldest son and heir, is deemed, in the East, the highest honor which can be conferred on a subject."[8] His actions were a symbol of his loyalty and commitment.

Loyalty isn't always a slam dunk.

I'm reminded of a story about a driver on the interstate who spotted a young man running along the shoulder of the road with three large pit bulls barking and running behind him. The kindly driver immediately pulled off onto the shoulder and backed his car up toward him. He reached over and opened the passenger side door and shouted toward the runner, "Quick! Get in the car!"

The young man ran toward the open door, the barking dogs still running behind him. Much to the driver's dismay, the dogs followed the young man right into the car, climbing all over him and into the back seat.

The driver yelled to the passenger, the dogs still barking loudly, "Are you okay?"

The runner replied over the barking, "Yes. Thanks for stopping, though. I'm heading to Atlanta, and it's not that easy to get a ride for me and all my dogs!"

What symbol of your loyalty will you offer a friend? Those very symbols can bring healing to any "loss of signal" along the lines of friendship.

Faithful in good or bad times. Are you as available in the bad times as you are in the good times? In the cartoon *Shoe*, Skyler holds up his report card and says, "I study all night and get a lousy C. And dumb Lenny lucks out an A!" His father replies, "You may as well get used to it, Skyler—life isn't fair. But then, death doesn't have a good track record either."[9]

Defends reputation. In a culture with a twisted law and order, where it's as if people are guilty until proven innocent, it's good to have a friend who will stand with you amidst the innuendos and indictments. Standing by isn't necessarily putting your blessing on someone's actions—it simply reminds them that your friendship is dependable and long-suffering (see Galatians 5:22-23).

Avoids negative talk. Are you a friend who provides the positive side? Zig Ziglar said, "I don't want to hang around people who brighten the room when they leave it; I want to hang around people who brighten the room when they enter it!"[10]

Non-judgmental. Do you have the tendency to make judgment calls like a line judge in a football game? Wait! Before you throw that flag, remember that you wouldn't necessarily want your own life to be put up on the stadium monitors during an "instant replay." Real friends are *teammates*, not referees.

Affirming. Ralph Waldo Emerson wrote, "The glory of friendship is not the outstretched hand, not the kindly smile, nor the joy of companionship; it is the spiritual inspiration that comes to one when he discovers that someone else believes in him and is willing to trust him."[11]

"Reality TV" is a misnomer. If you look behind the promos and read the credits, you'll see that most of it isn't real—it's staged. There's a common theme throughout the silliest scenarios: mishap and misery. Whether it's the "Housewives of Honolulu" or the "Cops of Calgary," the misfortunes of others result in fortunes for the producers. Submit a video of someone falling off a trampoline, tipping over a canoe, or running into a glass patio door, and you have a potential winner.

Jesus' Friends

Real friendship never lives off the spoils of another's loss. You'll never get ahead by a pattern of abandoning those who have been left behind. Jonathan sacrificed the kingdom to be David's friend; and David would have made the same sacrifice. "The Philistines pressed hard after Saul and his sons, and they killed his sons Jonathan, Abinadab and Malki-Shua" (1 Samuel 31:2).

Late network television news reporter Charles Osgood told the story of two ladies who lived in a convalescent center. Each had suffered an incapacitating stroke. Margaret's stroke restricted the use of her left side, while Ruth's stroke damaged her right side. Both of these ladies were accomplished pianists but had given up hope of ever playing again. The director of the center sat them down at a piano and encouraged them to play solo pieces together. They did, and a beautiful friendship developed.[12]

The friendship of Jonathan and David is a reminder of our friendship through faith with God's only son, the Lord Jesus

Christ. Oswald Chambers said, "True friendship is rare on earth. It means identifying with someone in thought, heart, and spirit. The whole experience of life is designed to enable us to enter in to this closest relationship with Jesus Christ."[13]

Jesus demonstrated His friendship for us by sacrificing His life.

As the Father has loved me, so have I loved you. Now remain in my love. If you obey my commands, you will remain in my love, just as I have obeyed my Father's commands and remain in his love. I have told you this so that my joy may be in you and that your joy may be complete. My command is this: Love each other as I have loved you. Greater love has no one than this, that he lay down his life for his friends. You are my friends if you do what I command. I no longer call you servants, because a servant does not know his master's business. Instead, I have called you friends, for everything that I learned from my Father I have made known to you. You did not choose me, but I chose you and appointed you to go and bear fruit—fruit that will last. Then the Father will give you whatever you ask in my name. This is my command: Love each other (*John 15:9-17*).

Jesus solidified His friendship with us by loving us when we were sinful (see John 3:16).

Near the Christmas season, a young student at a Christian school in West Africa listened carefully as his teacher explained why Christians give presents to each other on Christmas Day. "The gift is an expression of our joy over the birth of Jesus and our friendship for each other," she said.

When Christmas Day came, the student brought the teacher a seashell of lustrous beauty. "Where did you ever find such a beautiful shell?" the teacher asked.

The youth told her that there was only one spot where such extraordinary shells could be found. When he named the place, a certain bay several miles away, the teacher was left speech-less.

"Why, it's gorgeous—wonderful! But you shouldn't have gone all that way to get the gift for me."

His eyes brightening, the boy answered, "Long walk part of gift."[14]

God came from heaven to a manger, from a manger to a cross, from a cross to a grave, and from a grave back to heaven, to show us the friendship, love, and forgiveness that can be displayed in our earthly friendships—in our social networks.

We ask, "Why all this trouble, God?" And He would say to us, "Child, the long walk is part of the gift."

3

IF WEEDS ARE GROWING IN YOUR GARDEN, YOU'LL RUIN THE SQUASH
Real Forgiveness

🕮 Harriet and Edna were two unmarried elderly sisters who lived together for forty years. Their relationship, for the most part, was rather peaceful. But there was a boil beneath its surface that Walgreens's best ointment couldn't heal.

While in their twenties, Harriet had stolen Edna's boyfriend—a gangly, young assistant librarian whose hair parted restfully in the middle while several stood at attention in the back. Now, all these years later, Edna was in the hospital due to pneumonia that resulted from a chest cold she had caught at the church's recent yard sale.

The prognosis wasn't good, and Edna thought she might soon be standing at the pearly gates in her nightgown. Not one to take chances, she called for Harriet. "Harriet, I don't know whether I'm going to make it or not," she said. "Just to be sure, I think we need to talk about your taking Harold from me at that Sunday School picnic thirty-seven years, three months, and twelve hours ago."

Harriet not only remembered the event—the mention of Harold's name brought a slight flush to her well-powdered face. She replied, "Edna, I agree. We've been fussin' about that for too long. I'd be glad to get it settled."

Edna continued in the spirit of the moment: "Harriet, just in case this pneumonia wins the battle and I go home to be with Momma and Poppa, I want the Harold thing forgiven and forgotten." Harriet dutifully nodded her approval.

Edna than added a postscript: "But let me tell you one thing, sister: if I make it out of this hospital, the war ain't over!"

Relationships must have a solid foundation.

Solid Foundation

Relationships must have a solid foundation. If not, the weeds of wrong will kill them. And the rains of bad times, bad days, and bad attitudes will sweep them away like the house built on sand in Jesus' parable. How do you build a solid relationship foundation, and what are the materials? Let me share a few.

Mutual Respect

Recognizing the inherent worth of another individual is the first step in building mutual respect. When you affirm his or her God-given personality, gifts, and home environment in a positive and non-threatening way, you've started the building process.

United States President Gerald Ford once said, "Always demanding the best of oneself, living with honor, devoting one's talents and gifts to the benefit of others—these are the measures of success that endure when material things have passed away."[1]

Jesus told us to love others as we love ourselves. Building relationships within your social network begins with being at peace with *you*. It took me a good while to discover that God loved me for who I am and what I can do, rather than for how much I can be like someone else and do what he or she does.

Make this discovery: No one else has your gift and graces, even though they may seem similar to another's. You're as unique as your fingerprints. Only you can minister to a need in that certain and unique way. Rejoice over your "one-ness."

Courtesy

If you want to build a healthy relationship, treat every acquaintance with the same courtesy you would expect for yourself. An "eye for an eye" has a positive side to the coin. Watch these:

- Answer texts or e-mail in a timely manner.
- Don't procrastinate sending a thank-you note or returning a phone call.
- Keep your appointments.
- "As much as lieth in you," do what you promised.

Author Lillian Glass said that courteous people are conscious of their surroundings. "They are observant of manners, proper etiquette, and, most importantly, the feelings of others' mental and emotional states, and what crises they may be going through."[2]

Humor

If a spoonful of sugar can make the medicine go down, as Julie Andrews sang in the classic *The Sound of Music*, then a cupful of laughter can help someone digest a disaster. Maybe the only funny greeting card you can afford is the one on the fifty-percent markdown section at a dollar store, but that card could brighten the disturbing sameness in someone's life.

Maybe it's the West Virginia in me, but I don't think it ever hurts to share one of those "Have you heard the one about . . . ?" stories that can instantly ease a moment of tension. A good laugh is part of a good relationship and almost always puts you and another on common ground.

Mark Twain wrote in a *New York Times* article,

The quality of humor is not a personal or a national monopoly. It's as free as salvation, and, I am afraid, far more widely distributed. But it has its value, I think. The hard and sordid things of life are too hard and too sordid and too cruel for us to know and touch them year after year without some mitigating influence, some kindly veil to draw over them, from time to time, to blur the craggy outlines, and make the thorns less sharp and the cruelties less malignant.[3]

Generosity

United States President John F. Kennedy wowed the world with his "Ask not what your country can do for you—ask what you can do for your country" words. That what-you-can-do-for-your-country attitude has changed over the years. Now for the most part we live in an ask-me-what-you-can-do-for-me atmosphere.

But you and I can reverse that new normal by our generous deeds.

If I had to do the cooking I would need Rachel Ray to assist me in chopping the celery, but preparing a crock pot of soup—which would take considerably longer than thirty minutes—for a sick neighbor would probably help build an even better relationship than I already have with him or her.

Every single one of us has one of those "United Way" opportunities when we could respond to an immediate need with a gift. Just do it. It may cost you a couple of bucks, but it's an investment that will bring an even greater return.

I know firsthand that bags of groceries on the front porch of the Toler family turned a bleak childhood Christmas into one of beauty. I'll never forget that act of kindness. Somebody cared that my family didn't have any food at that time in our lives. Someone acted spontaneously to help. I've tried to spend a lifetime "paying forward" for that gift and have used it as an illustration for the blessing of generosity.

There's another building block for great relationships: forgiveness.

Forgiveness

Forgiveness is the root system of healthy human relationships. How we relate to others is based on trust in their character—on the sincerity of their affirmation and affection. If we allow the weeds of unforgiveness to wrap themselves around the roots, then personal or relational growth will cease. No matter their length or intensity, the health of our relationships is demonstrated by our willingness to forgive.

The health of our relationships is demonstrated
by our willingness to forgive.

When the star quarterback of a professional football team confessed to animal abuse a few years ago, the public outcry was one of rage and disbelief. When he apologized and asked his fans for forgiveness, many were skeptical, while others were ready to throw stones of revenge.

We shouldn't wonder when society struggles with forgiveness. The Church doesn't exactly have a stellar record on the subject. As Francis Schaffer once said, "If I am not willing to practice forgiveness, then the world has a right to question whether Christianity is true."[4] The Pharisees, religious leaders in Jesus' day, are Exhibit A.

If the Pharisees had their choice of seating in a courtroom, it would be in the "stoning" section. Known for their radical and sometimes hysterical stance on the fine print of the Mosaic law, they were willing to err on the side of judgment rather than mercy.

They were quick to sentence others for the slightest infractions while totally overlooking their own. Jesus talked about their seeing specks in the eyes of others while overlooking log jams in their own eyes.

Before you pass judgment on the group, think about your own seating preference: "stoning" or "non-stoning."

- How does the world see you?
- How does your social network see you?
- Are you known for your forgiving spirit, or are you known for living in a two-car "grudge"?

If biblical history is any clue, the Pharisees had some serious relational problems. Can you imagine what it would have been like to live with such self-righteous, unbending people? A Pharisee grand jury might be called to investigate the number of hand dips in the washing bowl before someone's meal at a Jerusalem potluck supper.

Stoning, the ultimate punishment of Bible times, was not uncommon. Interestingly, it is still used in some cultures. For the Pharisees, unforgiveness was their brand. An incident in ancient Palestine illustrates it:

Jesus went to the Mount of Olives. At dawn he appeared again in the temple courts, where all the people gathered around him, and he sat down to teach them. The teachers of the law and the Pharisees brought in a woman caught in adultery. They made her stand before the group and said to Jesus, "Teacher, this woman was caught in the act of adultery. In the Law Moses commanded us to stone such women. Now what do you say?" (*Mark 8:1-5*).

Obviously this infraction was more serious than the number of hand dips in a washing bowl. An infamous woman had broken a law of God and had abandoned the sanctity of her home.

She was guilty, caught in the very act.

The Pharisees had tried and convicted her in the courts of their minds, and now they wanted her to pay the ultimate price. But they were more intent on punishing the "doer" rather than condemning the "deed"—the sinner instead of the sin.

Look at what Jesus did. Instead of joining in their "rock concert," He went straight to the heart of the issue: only those who are perfect can demand judgment.

To Acquit or Not to Acquit

The Pharisees were playing the guilt card in order to build a case against Jesus. When a woman was caught in adultery, she was brought before Jesus and informed Him that the Law of Moses commanded that she be stoned. They asked Him what He had to say about that. The Son of Man responded by bending down and writing on the ground with His finger. When they kept on questioning Him, He stood up and said to them, "If any one of you is without sin, let him be the first to throw a stone at her" (John 8:8).

What did He write? Your guess is as good as mine. Since the adulteress broke the seventh commandment, some scholars think He scribbled a list of the Ten Commandments and then asked the Pharisees something akin to "Boys, how are you coming on those other nine?" Whatever it was, they got the message. The tiny thuds of dropped stones were followed by retreating shadows:

> At this, those who heard began to go away one at a time, the older ones first, until only Jesus was left, with the woman still standing there. Jesus straightened up and asked her, "Woman, where are they? Has no one condemned you?"

"No one, sir," she said. "Then neither do I condemn you," Jesus declared. "Go now and leave your life of sin" (John 8:9-11).

To Forgive or Not Forgive

"When Jesus spoke again to the people, he said, 'I am the light of the world. Whoever follows me will never walk in darkness, but will have the light of life'" (John 8:12). Jesus brought the "light" of holy living to the woman and the remaining bystanders. His actions also taught us a lot about the principles of His forgiveness:

1. His forgiveness is "grace-full."

However, to the man who does not work but trusts God who justifies the wicked, his faith is credited as righteousness. David says the same thing when he speaks of the blessedness of the man to whom God credits righteousness apart from works: "Blessed are they whose transgressions are forgiven, whose sins are covered. Blessed is the man whose sin the Lord will never count against him" (*Romans 4:5-8*).

A beautiful gospel song says of the sin we inherited from Adam and Eve,

> *The guilty pair, bowed down with care,*
> *God gave His Son to win;*
> *His erring child He reconciled,*
> *And pardoned from his sin.*

> *O love of God, how rich and pure!*
> *How measureless and strong!*
> *It shall forevermore endure—*
> *The saints' and angels' song!*
> —Frederick M. Lehman

When you forgive another, you're celebrating the forgiveness of Christ. "The Word became flesh and made his dwelling among us. We have seen his glory, the glory of the One and

Only, who came from the Father, full of grace and truth" (John 1:14). Forgiveness is an act of grace—one that's born in the sacrifice of God's Son. In one sense, to withhold forgiveness is to blaspheme the atoning work of the Cross. I know that's heavy, but it's true.

You were guilty, and Christ was guiltless; yet He borrowed your guilt and took it to Calvary. Because you were forgiven, you can forgive. Do you hear His voice, "Forgive"? Listen carefully—it's a matter of life or death spiritually and relationally.

2. His forgiveness is not based on the degree of our disobedience.

If we confess our sins, he is faithful and just and will forgive us our sins and purify us from all unrighteousness (*1 John 1:9*).

Did you catch that word *all?* Sin doesn't have a Richter scale like earthquakes. One is just as bad as another, and all are tragic in the eyes of a holy God (see Habakuk 1:13). Forgiveness isn't measured either. One action may be more severe than another, but no matter the action, the *actor* is a candidate for reconciliation.

3. His forgiveness is forgetful.

Ah, forgetfulness—the rite of passage into middle age!

The grandchild is already climbing into the toddler seat in the back seat of your van, having spanned the distance from the kitchen to the vehicle in a time that would make an Olympic runner weep with envy.

The repairman just called and said the part for your washing machine would be here in just three more years. You just opened the note from your daughter that came last week, only to discover that she and her four kids would be coming to stay with you for the summer—and the blessed arrival is only three days away.

Suddenly you remember your grandchild is absent. Gone, just like in the *Left Behind* books and movies! And you're looking for your keys. And you can't remember if you left them on the table beside your stack of coupons from the drugstore or on the broken washing machine.

It hits you. You remember that at times it seems as if your memory loses its charge like a cheap battery in a junkyard pickup truck.

In the positive, forgetting is one of the chosen character qualities of the Divine. Out of His lovingkindness, He has chosen to forget some things. For example, God chose to limit His remembrance of our pasts.

If you have a digital camera, you've probably had to put a picture or two into the "digital dumpster"—usually a garbage can icon on the viewing screen picturing that inner place on your device reserved for out-of-focus or dog's-tail-in-the-frame photos. Thankfully, the camera's creators usually put an "Are you sure?" symbol on the menu, or you might accidentally lose a picture of a grandson playing his first T-ball game.

God was sure. The sins of our past that are forgiven through saving faith in the Lord Jesus Christ are purposefully deleted. You can *choose* to forget. You can put it in the *delete folder*.

4. His forgiveness is complete.

The adulteress in Jesus' parable remains nameless. Was her infamy known in the community? Probably. Could her name have been listed in the Scriptures—like Rahab the harlot? Certainly. But Jesus promised her a clean résumé. She would never have to include the word *adulteress* again. I think the omission of her name in the Scripture credits was symbolic of God's forgiveness.

There won't be any storage cards in heaven. You'll have to clean your hard drive on this side of the gate. God has a perfect antidote: forgiveness. "'Come now, let us reason together,' says the LORD. 'Though your sins are like scarlet, they shall be as white as snow; though they are red as crimson, they shall be like wool'" (Isaiah 1:18).

The Game Plan: Forgiving Living

You might say, "I know forgiveness is in the rules, but how do you play the game?" Thankfully, our Player-Coach, Jesus, doesn't just *tell* us how to do things from the sidelines of heaven. By His Holy Spirit, He's on the field playing the game of life *with* us.

His past performance put Him in the Hall of Fame; but He wasn't content to rest on His laurels—He kept playing as well as coaching. His Holy Spirit indwells us at the point of our conversion and continues to point us to the principles and actions He displayed on earth. Forgiveness simply models the life and example of Jesus Christ.

What is the game plan?

First, remember where He brought you from. The familiar song reminds us, "I once was lost but now am found, was blind but now I see." Paul said, "Remember that at that time you were separate from Christ, excluded from citizenship in Israel and foreigners to the covenants of the promise, without hope and without God in the world" (Ephesians 2:12). Once you were in the stands—now you're on the team. In other words, once you were only remotely familiar with the team and the coach, but now you're intimately acquainted with Him—you belong on the team (John 1:12). As a result, you were brought into the knowledge of forgiving living.

Forgiveness simply models the life
and example of Jesus Christ.

I love to play tennis, but some people don't want to be involved in a game where "love" means "nothing." Before I played, I was a good bystander. I could have lettered in popcorn and soft drinks. But I never knew how much I liked tennis until I got on the tennis court. Playing on the court was a lot more fun than sitting in the stands. I was learning by doing.

Remember: you're now part of the team. Your understanding of forgiving living comes from your playing time and the constant presence and instruction of your Player-Coach.

Second, ask God to refresh your memory. Forgiving living doesn't just happen because of an intervention—it happens also because of spiritual introspection. Jesus said, "When you stand praying, if you hold anything against anyone, forgive him, so that your Father in heaven may forgive you your sins. But if you do not forgive, neither will your Father who is in heaven forgive your sins" (Mark 11:25-26). I presume—and I hope—that those pilots who guide the airplanes I fly on regularly have thoroughly gone over their flight deck checklist. Believe me—

- I want to be sure that every light is lit.
- I want to know that every button is pushed.
- I want to know that every arrow on the instrument panel points in the right direction.

Why? I know that contrary to what the flight attendant may say or the catastrophe catalog sheet in the seat pocket may read, in the event of a crash landing it will be impossible to put my head on my knees! There isn't enough room for a crow's foot between the seat rows on an airplane!

The psalmist David prayed, "Search me, O God, and know my heart" (Psalm 139:23). He was going through his spiritual checklist. He wanted to be sure the lights were lit, the buttons were pushed, and the dials were all pointing in the right direction. Forgiving living does the same thing. It opens itself up to the Holy Spirit searching to see if the last weeds in the garden of the heart have been pulled. As you know, weeding is a continuing process.

Ask God to refresh your memory.

Third, quit rehearsing your personal failures. In other words, let it go! You've probably seen an intervention segment on a television show. The host or family and friends confront someone with an addiction or some other behavioral problem. Prepared statements are read, tears flow, and the person on the hot seat has to make a decision about changing his or her ways. It's good television, but it's time wasted until the addict decides to put past behavior behind him or her and start living in a new and better way.

The apostle Paul said, "One thing I do: Forgetting what is behind and straining toward what is ahead, I press on toward the goal" (Philippians 3:13-14). Linda and I have several friends who play professional baseball. We've watched them develop their athletic skills over the years. They wouldn't be where they are in their careers if they had focused on every strikeout, missed catch, or running error. They focused on the goal—on winning, on pitching a great game, or making a game-saving play.

A redneck came to the city for a bottle collector convention. When he checked into the swanky hotel in the heart of downtown, he was asked to sign his name on the guest register. He didn't have a pen, and he didn't want to get any germs off the desk pen, so he went back to his truck, where two hotel valets were tossing a coin to see who would park it, and got a black permanent marker out of the glove box. He remembered he put one in there after making a "Dandelion Greens" sign for his stall at the farmer's market.

"Got a pen," he said to the hostess at the hotel counter. "Where do you want me to sign?"

She pointed to a line in the register and said, "Put your full name on that line."

With two swipes of the black marker he made an X that took up five lines in the register.

"May I ask why you didn't put your name on the lines?" the startled hostess asked.

"Ma'am, I'm new in this town. If I use my real name someone might steal my identity."

The problem wasn't an identity theft. It was a literacy problem—one he had been trying to cover for years.

You'll never develop a forgiving living attitude if you're not able to forgive yourself. Even at this moment you can rely on the promised forgiveness of the one who cannot and will not lie. If God said He will forgive you, you can be sure that when you ask, He will.

Fourth, release the spirit of unforgiveness. Unforgiveness is like wearing a hooded sweatshirt over a wool sweater on an August day in Oklahoma. It's uncomfortable, unsightly, and will likely cause considerable outbreaks of perspiration.

It's also restrictive—especially if you're going to play tennis. Granted, the layered look comes in and out of style, but in an athletic competition, less is more. Extra clothing adds more weight and hinders your range of motion.

It's the same in your spiritual life—especially as it relates to your relationship with others. The Bible says, "Get rid of all bitterness, rage and anger, brawling and slander, along with every form of malice. Be kind and compassionate to one another, forgiving each other, just as in Christ God forgave you" (Ephesians 4:31-32).

What are you "wearing" that's unsightly for a Christian and that hinders your spiritual motion? Could it be an unforgiving spirit? "God did not give us a spirit of timidity, but a spirit of power, of love and of self-discipline" (2 Timothy 2:7). Surely if there's a spirit of fear, there's also a spirit of unforgiveness. Get rid of it; release it to Christ in prayer.

Fifth, forgive before you're asked. Developing forgiving living means to forgive proactively. Civil rights leader Martin Luther King Jr. said, "Forgiveness is not an occasional act; it is a permanent attitude."[5]

Extending forgiveness at the outset of a relationship problem is a lot easier than waiting until the problem develops into bitterness. Jesus modeled that in His behavior on the Cross.

"Jesus said, 'Father, forgive them, for they do not know what they are doing.' And they divided up his clothes by casting lots" (Luke 23:34).

Totally in character, Jesus of Nazareth took the first step of mercy. He was the guiltless one. His cross wasn't His own—it was forced upon Him, but He took it willingly. Out of His heart of love, He proactively offered reconciliation.

Real Forgiveness

An online news item proved that differences should be settled long before they escalate into air warfare. A couple in a state way below the Mason-Dixon Line got into an altercation, and they were both charged with assault and battery. Their weapons of choice will probably long be remembered in the annals of law enforcement. Not being able to settle their differences with words, they chose to throw Cheetos at one another. That's right, those puffy, Styrofoamy, snack food items were used as projectiles in their moment of anger.

Maybe you can't imagine a relationship so broken that people resort to throwing snack food at each other. Or maybe you can. Either way, you must know that a spirit of forgiveness is a healing factor in broken bonds and personal hurts. Real forgiveness is a solution to the problem of weeds choking out the growth of your relationships. It is Christlike, practical, and absolutely necessary for your peace of mind.

Where will it start?

It must always start with you. Until you decide to bring the character and characteristics of Christ into your relational situations, you'll never know healing. But once you do, you'll begin to relate to others in a positive and affirming way.

Forgiving—and forgetting—will give you a better life perspective. In my book *God Is Never Late; He's Seldom Early; He's Always Right On Time* I tell the story of an overbooked airline flight out of Baltimore. One agent was trying to answer all the passenger questions, talk to her supervisor, and read the monitor at the same time.

One passenger fox-trotted to the front of the line of people at the counter and confronted the agent. Slamming his fist on the counter, he exclaimed, "I have to be on this flight! And it has to be in first class!"

The agent replied, "I'm sorry, sir. I'll be happy to help you, but I have to take care of these folks first."

Unimpressed, the passenger responded in a booming voice, "Young lady, do you have any idea who I am?"

Without hesitating, the gate agent smiled and picked up her public address microphone. "May I have your attention, please?" she broadcast through the terminal. "We have a passenger at Gate 37 who does not know who he is. If anyone can help, please come to the gate."[6]

Do you know who you are? A forgiven child of God? I pray so. And I know that in that wonderful state of grace you will find strength and initiative to be a forgiver, to let Christ's redemptive mercy flood your heart—as well as your relationships.

4

IF YOU CAN'T STAND THE HEAT, DON'T MOVE TO THE DESERT
Real Faith

A man riding a camel took a wrong turn in Cairo and ended up lost in the desert. Riding for miles across the sun-drenched sand, he searched for signs of life. His supplies were running low when all of a sudden his camel dropped to its knees and expired from a heat stroke. Now on foot, he desperately sought refuge from the scorching sun, and most importantly, he sought water. To his surprise, he came across a refreshment stand with a man sitting on a folding chair beside it reading the *Cairo Times*.

"Thank goodness I found you!" the man cried. "I need some water!"

"I'm sorry, sir," the salesman replied, looking up. "I just sold the last bottle of water to a caravan of teens on a missions trip."

"No!" the thirsty camel rider said. "Do you have anything else?"

The man replied, "We sell soft drinks—Coke, root beer, Pepsi—"

The traveler interrupted—"Pepsi! Large!"

"Sorry," the owner said, "No more Pepsi. In fact, I'm all out of soft drinks."

"What exactly *do* you have?"

The owner reached under the counter and pulled out a handful of silk ties. "I have lots of ties—pure silk, imported from Taiwan—only $25."

"What am I going to do with a tie?" the man asked angrily.

"Might come in handy some day," the owner replied.

"Ties!" the traveler muttered as he abruptly left the refreshment stand and continued walking across the desert sand, "Why do I need with a tie?"

Several hours later he saw a building in the distance. *Water!* he thought as he walked toward it.

Finally he reached the building. It was a restaurant. The huge neon sign over the restaurant said, "EDDIE'S FIVE-STAR DINING."

Amazed and thirstier than ever, he approached the front door and read the menu displayed in a case near the door. Overjoyed to see bottled Perrier water on the menu, he walked in and was immediately met by the maitre d'.

The tuxedoed man said, "I'm sorry, sir, but you can't come in here without a tie."

Now, I don't know if your camel has ever expired or if you've ever been lost in the desert, but what the traveler found out was the same we all will find out sooner or later: deserts are full of surprises.

Perhaps none could testify to that fact any more than the "first couple of the covenant," Abraham and Sarah. Their marriage relationship was the proving ground of their faith. When they heard that classic question "Wilt thou?" they didn't wilt. They answered in the awesome affirmative. Their faith in God and in each other was the kind that prevents the turning of matrimony into a *misery*.

Several important factors can been seen here.

1. Abraham and Sarah faced uncertainty with confidence for the future.

For years their life was routine, as routine as it could be in Bible times. For Abraham and his family, their "house" was probably a tent made from goat's hair. Bread was the main course for all meals—and doubled as their utensils, sopping and spooning other foods from a common kettle. At night, oil lamps dimly lit their tents. They probably went to bed very early, after sitting by a fire fueled by animal dung, and slept on mattresses filled with wool or straw, covered by goat's hair blankets.

The morning brought tiring work—picking olives, planting crops, fighting drought, or tending sheep. Any trip to a neighboring small town meant walking on foot or riding beasts of burden along tiny trails.[1]

Uncertainty was a way of life for Abraham and his family. Whether it was dangerous animals or marauding enemies, their homeland security director had his hands full. And who knows what the terror threat level might have been when a pack of wolves got hungry after a day of tanning on the rocks and ledges near their camp?

If you're a fan of classic television shows, you've probably seen a rerun or two of *I Love Lucy*. Talk about surprises. When Desi Arnaz walked through the front door of that television set and announced, "Lucy—I'm home!" it was anyone's guess as to what might happen next—and what the beloved Lucille Ball might be up to.

Flash back hundreds of years to a funny-sounding country called "Ur." A great man of Bible times named Abraham walks through the tent door and announces, "Sarah—I'm home!" Little did she know what a surprise he had in store.

"How did your day go, husband?" she greeted.

"Oh, fine," he said. "The rush-hour traffic was pretty bad, though. There was a camel-and-donkey wreck downtown. Some jackass went through a stop sign and broadsided a dromedary."

"I'm sorry, husband," she responded, "Any other news?"

"Well, yes." Abraham said as he searched for the remote. "God told me to move the family out of Ur and head for 'the Promised Land.'"

"Move? Where?" she replied, looking as if she had just choked on a pomegranate

With a fake smile, Abraham said, "'The Promised Land.' I don't know much about it, but God told me to move there, so that's where we must go."

Sarah's smile was even more plastic. "You don't know much about it?"

"No, but I do know that whenever God has asked us to do something, there has always been a positive result."

There was a slight pause. "O-o-o-k-a-ay—but could you just give me a few more details about that conversation with God?"

Here are the details:

> The LORD had said to Abram, "Leave your country, your people and your father's household and go to the land I will show you. I will make you into a great nation and I will bless you; I will make your name great, and you will be a blessing. I will bless those who bless you, and whoever curses you I will curse; and all peoples on earth will be blessed through you" (*Genesis 12:1-3*).

What happened next would be the difference between faith and *real faith*. Abraham and Sarah were walking the line. What was on the line?

• Trust
• Character
• Obedience
• Respect

- Love

Interestingly, some of the very things that define a real relationship were on the line.

At a conference of church custodians there was a discussion about getting rid of mice. Several solutions were offered. One custodian said, "We put out some mousetraps with the finest cheese in town in them, but it didn't help. About a week later, they came right back.

Another custodian responded, "We locked a cat in the church at night. We didn't have a mouse problem for several months, but eventually they came back."

They asked a third custodian how he had solved the problem.

"Easy. We put 'em in a membership class; then six weeks later, the pastor baptized them. That was ten years ago. Haven't seen 'em since."[2]

Faith, of course, is focused on God, His holy character, and His mercy and grace. It is the engine of the Christian life. Without it, even the "religious" are using a spiritual skateboard to try to push their way to heaven.

Without faith it is impossible to please God, because anyone who comes to him must believe that he exists and that he rewards those who earnestly seek him (*Hebrews 11:5*).

For sure, faith isn't for the showroom—it's for the *workroom*. It works itself out in our everyday activities and relationships.

Now someone may argue, "Some people have faith; others have good deeds." I say, "I can't see your faith if you don't have good deeds, but I will show you my faith through my good deeds "(*James 2:18, NLT*).

Otis Skillings wrote a descriptive song that speaks of "the bond of love" that Christian believers experience. When the philosophy of truth digs deeply into your heart, you'll have an even greater insight into real relationships.

If faith is the engine of a relationship, then the Spirit of Christ is the fuel (see Romans 8:5-11). Paul gave us a litmus test for Christ-fueled faith:

Is there any encouragement from belonging to Christ? Any comfort from his love? Any fellowship together in the Spirit? Are your hearts tender and sympathetic? Then make me truly happy by agreeing wholeheartedly with each other, loving one another, and working together with one heart and purpose. Don't be selfish; don't live to make a good impression on others. Be humble, thinking of others as better than yourself. Don't think only about your own affairs, but be interested in others, too, and what they are doing (*Philippians 2:1-4, NLT*).

What does that look like on a bio? The same as in Abraham's life:

- Trust
- Character
- Obedience
- Respect
- Love

Abram modeled it. Was he focused on God? "And the scripture was fulfilled that says, 'Abraham believed God, and it was credited to him as righteousness,' and he was called God's friend" (James 2:23).

I suppose if you were going to be envious about anyone's guest list, you would think of Abraham's. He's having a dinner for twelve, and guess who's invited? That's right: the One who created the food—and I don't mean an "Iron Chef" either!

Imagine having such great faith that God declares you a friend! It wasn't just in the fact that he was willing to pull up stakes—literally—and move. It was because Abraham built his whole life around his faith. It wasn't mere lip service. He demonstrated it.

Trust: So Abram [name later changed to Abraham] left, as the LORD had told him; and Lot [his nephew] went with him. Abram was seventy-five years old when he set out from Haran.

Character: He took his wife Sarai [name later changed to Sarah], his nephew Lot, all the possessions they had accumulated and the people they had acquired in Haran, and they set out for the land of Canaan, and they arrived there.

Obedience: Abram traveled through the land as far as the site of the great tree of Moreh at Shechem. At that time the Canaanites were in the land. The LORD appeared to Abram and said, "To your offspring I will give this land."

Respect: So he built an altar there to the LORD, who had appeared to him.

Love: From there he went on toward the hills east of Bethel and pitched his tent, with Bethel on the west and Ai on the east. There he built an altar to the LORD and called on the name of the LORD. Then Abram set out and continued toward the Negev (*Genesis 12:1-9, bold headings added*).

This wasn't a journey of convenience; it was a journey of commitment. Abraham's love for God drove him on. There wasn't a Hilton Hotel in sight. The desert wasn't air conditioned. There was no Wal-Mart where they could pick up camping supplies.

Abraham and Sarah weren't singing "Happy Trails to You," like Roy Rogers and Dale Evans in a fifties western movie, riding off into the golden sunset. These would be tough travel days. But they had made an eternal commitment to an eternal God.

Perhaps you can feel their pain. Perhaps your days have been long, your circumstances have been difficult, or your relationships have been strained by the times. In the book I co-authored with Debra White Smith, *The Harder I Laugh, the*

Deeper I Hurt, I outline the strategy I used when uncertainty invaded my home as a child after my father's accidental death:

- **Be honest about your hurts.** Admit them as an act of faith in God's healing.
- **Thank God for His presence in the midst of the pain.** Suffering draws us closer to God.
- **Take refuge in the love of your family.** Confide your fears to them. Let them be your rock of acceptance.
- **Spend some time alone with God.** Find a hideaway from the "noonday heat."
- **Spend some time with a close friend.** Share a cup of coffee along with sharing your burdens.
- **Spend some time with a good book.** God has allowed others to go through adversity. Learn from them.
- **Look ahead.** Plan for a positive future. Think in terms of the "later on."
- **Write it down.** Keep a spiritual journal. Write down the promises God gives you the Bible.
- **Make an attitude adjustment.** Choose to survive.
- **Minister to others.** Nothing will help you bear the load you are carrying more than helping someone else carry their load.[3]

2. Abraham and Sarah leaned on the covenant in the face of the conflict.

Abraham and Sarah were people of the covenant. "The word of the LORD came to Abram in a vision: 'Do not be afraid, Abram. I am your shield, your very great reward'" (Genesis 15:1). Notice the key words: "the word of the Lord;" "Do not be afraid;" "I am your shield"—strong words, action words, promising words. It was the second of God's great covenants with His people. Like the first (see Genesis 9), this was a blanket policy: it covered all God's children—forever. That includes you and me.

The second person in this real relationship was Abraham's wife, Sarah. Not surprisingly, she modeled the same "real relationships" qualities as her husband.

- Trust
- Character
- Obedience
- Respect
- Love

Hers was a history of faithfulness to God and to her relationship with Abraham. "It was by faith that Sarah together with Abraham was able to have a child, even though they were too old and Sarah was barren. Abraham believed that God would keep his promise" (Hebrews 11:11, NLT).

For Sarah, this was an extreme test. In the context of her times, bearing children validated her femininity—her value to her husband. An infertile woman was looked upon with pity. Sarah could have blamed God for the low opinion others had of her. After all, He was the one who promised them children. She could have turned her back on Him and made it more difficult for Abraham to believe. But it doesn't seem she did so.

Though she struggled with God's timeline and even laughed out loud at the thought of having a child at her advanced age, she didn't let the rope of her faith go entirely slack. She believed God.

I like the story of the one-hundred-thirty-pound young man who applied for a job as a lumberjack. Surrounded by Hulk Hogan-type lumberjacks at the company office shack, the young man, dressed in denim overalls that looked as if they were three sizes too big and a white T-shirt that made his arms look like dead twigs hanging from an aging branch, approached the supervisor. "I'd like to be one of your lumberjacks, sir."

The supervisor, whose muscular physique stretched the plaid wool shirt he was wearing, took one look at the job applicant and laughed. "Son, you look like you couldn't bend a cotton swab! Have you ever tried anything like this before?"

Standing as tall as he could, the slight lumberjack wannabe replied, "Of course."

"I'll tell you what," the boss said. "We're a man short today. I'll give you an axe; you go out to those woods and cut me down a redwood."

Thirty minutes later, the young man reported back: "I cut down that redwood tree and split it up into a lumber pile."

The burly boss was stunned. "Where did you learn how to cut trees like that?"

"The Mojave Desert," the boy said.

"The desert?" the boss replied. "You cut trees down in a *desert?*"

The young man explained confidently, "It's a desert now. But before I got the job, it was a forest!"

It was that kind of confidence that Abraham had when he accepted God's job.

> By faith Abraham, when called to go to a place he would later receive as his inheritance, obeyed and went, even though he did not know where he was going. By faith he made his home in the promised land like a stranger in a foreign country; he lived in tents, as did Isaac and Jacob, who were heirs with him of the same promise. For he was looking forward to the city with foundations, whose architect and builder is God (*Hebrews 11:8-10*).

Sure, the assignment was tough. Sure, the times were working against them. But Abraham and Sarah believed in each other, and together they believed in their God.

They not only flipped the forest—they flipped the desert!

• They survived the adversities of living in a wilderness.

• They had their first biological child at the stage in life when most couples welcome their great- and great-great-grandchildren.

- They faced hostile kings and barren landscapes.
- They faced a selfish family member and pagan neighbors.
- They met the challenges and triumphed over their difficulties. And today the entire nation of Israel traces its origin to a son who would born to them: Isaac.

By faith Abraham, even though he was past age—and Sarah herself was barren—was enabled to become a father because he considered him faithful who had made the promise. And so from this one man, and he as good as dead, came descendants as numerous as the stars in the sky and as countless as the sand on the seashore (*Hebrews 11:11-12*).

3. Abraham and Sarah saw loss as one of God's answers.

Have there been times in your life or relationships when it seemed as if God wasn't listening, when questions played on your soul louder than a heavy metal band with a new sound system?

Sometimes God's answers aren't that obvious. Sometimes they crawl silently across the monitor of your heart like headlines on a news channel, and you don't notice because you're too busy watching the bigger picture.

Sooner or later, you or your partner will discover that even loss can be one of God's answers. Sometimes He simply does *nothing* to stop the awful effects of Adam's sin and resulting devastation to humanity. Abraham faced a devastating situation.

Not only did Abraham relate to his wife with faith, but he also related to his children with faith. Abraham was a player in what is arguably the most intense testing times in the Bible. The son of promise, Isaac, was the apple of Abraham's eye. Imagine his feelings when God tested Abraham by asking him to offer his son on an altar of sacrifice (see Genesis 22:1-14).

- The Genesis account recalls the lonely walk toward the mountain of sacrifice, the gut-wrenching question from Isaac about what sacrifice would be offered.

• The Genesis account shows the obedience of Isaac when Abraham bound him and placed him on the altar.

• The Genesis account shows the response of a loving God in offering a substitute ram just as the knife was raised over Isaac.

The New Testament writer reflects as if he were reading a biography of Abraham during his induction into "the Faith Hall of Fame":

By faith Abraham, when God tested him, offered Isaac as a sacrifice. He who had received the promises was about to sacrifice his one and only son, even though God had said to him, "It is through Isaac that your offspring will be reckoned." Abraham reasoned that God could raise the dead, and figuratively speaking, he did receive Isaac back from death (*Hebrews 11:17-19*).

Abraham trusted God with the son of promise—Isaac. Though he had waited decades for this boy, he had trusted God longer. He dared to believe that even death could not extinguish the promise of many descendants God had made to him on a starry desert night.

God's vindication of Sarah's womanhood would be firm and lasting no matter how impossible it seemed at the moment. God kept His word—Sarah has been validated down through time with every Jewish birth.

Even losses are turned to gains in God's hands. Sometimes you'll never understand the dynamics of living on the earth; why birth is followed by pain or death, or why companionship is followed by separation.

Bonnie Barrows Thomas wrote,

Thank You, Father, for these tears that have carried me to the depths of Your love. How could I have known Your fullness without the emptiness, Your acceptance without the rejection, Your forgiveness without any failure, our togetherness without that dreadful loneliness? You have brought me to Gethsemane, and oh, the joy of finding You already there![4]

4. Abraham and Sarah were empowered by the strengths of their partners.

Obvious or not, recognized or suppressed, God has gifted marriage partners with strengths that offset the other's weaknesses. "So in Christ we who are many form one body, and each member belongs to all the others. We have different gifts, according to the grace given us. If a man's gift is prophesying, let him use it in proportion to his faith" (Romans 12:5-6).

In a *real* relationship, one person supports the other by using his or her abilities to empower the other. For example, an outgoing person may take the lead when attending a function that includes the other. One's courage offsets the other's fears. One's confidence bolsters the other's insecurities. How do you determine when to offer your strengths?

Hyrum Smith writes about football. He says that most quarterbacks receive their plays from the sidelines. But sometimes the quarterback and team come to the line, the quarterback sweeps the defense, and he spots a weakness. That calls for an "audible"—the quarterback makes a split-second decision based on his observation. Smith writes, "When this happens, you will see the quarterback as he approaches the center to receive the ball, yell out a whole new play based on his assessment of what the team is now facing from the defense."[5]

In a world in which we face the scorching heat of cynicism and the arid winds of cultural shifts, finding a bit of hope is as infrequent as a palm tree-lined oasis in the desert.

The events of our political and social world blow with gale force, whipping the sands of confusion into our relationships. As the tent flaps dance in the wind, we face the same question Abraham and Sarah faced—how to interface family and faith.

Savings and Trust

It's all about trust—believing in the God who can make anything come to pass and daring to act on it. What if Abraham had given up somewhere in the Negev? Instead of crossing the next dune, he could have circled the camels and pounded down the tent stakes for the last time. There would be no Canaan, no Isaac, and no Israel. An archeological dig might find the bones of Abraham, but he would not have died in faith.

Instead, he chose to live a life marked by faith, he drew his wife and sons into his faith with him, and he left a legacy of faith that has imprinted everyone who comes from his lineage. You can hear it in the voices as they chant, "Hear, O Israel, the Lord our God is one."

Abraham related to his family through faith. How can we do the same?

- Have genuine devotion. (See Genesis 17:1. Abraham lived out his faith authentically.)
- Make faith a family commitment. (See Genesis 17:26; 21:4. Abraham brought his sons into the covenant.)
- Keep relationships alive even when there are separations. (See Genesis 25:9. Both sons buried Abraham. There must have been ongoing relationship between Abraham and Ishmael.)
- Be honest about the challenges of faith. (See Genesis 22:7-8. Abraham openly took Isaac to the mountain of sacrifice and didn't shy from his question.)

God will provide even in the desert if we trust Him for the directions. There's no better way to face life or nurture relationships than in the desert if you have a faith that leads the way.

Someone once said, "What makes the desert beautiful is that somewhere it hides a well."

5

IF YOU BURY THE HATCHET, SELL YOUR METAL DETECTOR
Real Conflict

⟫ A friend of mine shared a grandson story. Being a grandfather myself, I'm always ready to hear a grandson story (as long as I get my turn!).

He said he overhead two of his grandsons arguing. One suddenly blurted out to the other, "I hate you!" My friend rushed into the room and pulled the offender aside. "Son, you're never supposed to say that. Hating someone is a sin and could keep you out of heaven!"

Expecting a little remorse and perhaps some repentance, Grandfather was surprised to hear the offender's response: "If he's going to keep me out of heaven, I hate him even *more*!"

1. Conflict is as common as a thrown shoe.

History has a way of including the odd along with the inevitable. And often presidents, princes, and kings become a historical focal point. President George W. Bush not only became a focal point—he also became a target for a shoe-thrower during an overseas press conference. The media had a field day with the "sole" of the incident, but who knows whether or not a "shoe salesman" had ties to that fit seen 'round the world?

Ever since Cain and Abel, the first- and second-born of Adam and Eve, relationships have been prone to conflict. Theirs was the Super Bowl of conflicts. So, upset with what his brother Abel put into the offering plate, Cain murdered him (see Genesis 4:1-26).

You might be the treasurer of your church or organization. You probably haven't considered murder, but the puny results of some offering or collection of dues might have tempted you to give someone a first-degree tongue-lashing! Instead, you might do as I've seen in some churches: if the first offering didn't bring in enough, they take another one.

Fact is, whether you're a treasurer or not, conflicts are one of the dangers of real relationships. Nature proves it. For example, studies show that if you put a minimum of two siblings in the back seat of a vehicle, buckle them in, and drive to Canada, there will be at least one conflict in that vehicle before the trip is over—even if you already live in Canada.

A friend of mine tells me about the time his father pulled to the side of the road and kept the promise "If you two don't stop fighting, I'm going to stop this car and give you a whuppin'!" He said his father kept his promise—and even stopped the car on a bridge! (He also said the fight was over by the time the father had opened the driver's side door.)

The effect of conflicts in a relationship may vary, but the great common denominator is that every relationship will experience conflict at some level.

When does conflict cross the "reasonable" line? A cable news channel reported an interesting disagreement on their web site. It seems that a husband and wife in Texas had an escalating fuss over jewelry. Police reports said he took back some jewelry he had given to her, and she didn't take too kindly to that. Suddenly the bangles became a storm cloud on the horizon of their future.

Her solution to the situation?

She took his prize goldfish and put them into the frying pan. That's right—the upset wife took Goldie and Goldie's friend, Pam, to a fish fry, where they were the guests of honor.[1]

Now most parents know what it is to send a couple of goldfish on a porcelain cruise before leaving on a vacation, but this was carrying fish "boarding" to a new level—a lower level.

Reasons for conflict are quite obvious: we have unique perspectives and personal opinions. Inside all of us is a "town hall meeting"—with the tendency to think that it's always our turn at the microphone. What is the DNA of those perspectives and opinions?

- *Our physiology:* We have the "expression genes" of our parentage. For some, there's plenty of "bark" on the family tree. We may come from families that are very expressive about their perspectives, while others simply keep their opinions to themselves. For example, you may be in the midst of a lengthy debate over adding an upgrade to your basic cable service. Accidentally—or on purpose—the *you* word pops out of your mouth. Your significant other will respond according to the way he or she was raised.

- *Environment:* We come from homes where opinions were either denied or discussed. "Children should be seen and not heard" was a common philosophy of past generations. The new normal seems to be quite the opposite, where children often hold center stage while their parents cringe and gasp behind the stage curtains. Again, how you react depends largely on how you were raised.

- *Circumstances:* We react based on past or present extremes. Why do some situations cause us to turn icy cold or sizzling hot? Think about the déjà vu factor. You face a tense situation, and all of a sudden a situation from your past plays on your mind like a DVD segment. "Been there, done that!" If the situation was unpleasant or threatening to your self-esteem, you'll probably tense up—and maybe boil over—based on a similar situation from your past.

- *Identity:* We express ourselves in keeping with our self-image. Some conflicts threaten the person we perceive ourselves to be: Leader, winner, or authority. Situations mirror our reflections, often resulting in a conscious or unconscious struggle for recognition.

- *Motivation:* We express ourselves in keeping with our wants or needs. Most of us would choose affirmation over defamation any day of the week. It goes all the way back to that pencil prize in Sunday School class. Remember the pride you felt when your teacher pulled a trick Bible question and you were the only one in your class who remembered that Hezekiah isn't a book of the Old Testament?

God's Word addresses the real issues of life, and relationship is one of the major themes. And to give an accurate portrait of what relationships are like, conflict is addressed.

2. Conflict doesn't have a post office box.

Conflict is as itinerant as a flea at a dog show. It doesn't have a sociological, theological, or economical address. It doesn't even have a toll-free number where you can get further information. It happens everywhere, to anyone, at any time.

It happened at Antioch. It seems that some first-century church folks in the city approximately three hundred miles north of Jerusalem "heard a discouraging word" that shook their faith like a hankie in a Pentecostal revival.

Christian "teachers" from Jerusalem were trying to convince them that Jewish ceremonial traditions should be included in Christianity. Paul and Barnabas, Christian missionaries and church leaders, had a different perspective, which resulted in a public conflict. "This brought Paul and Barnabas into sharp dispute and debate with them" (Acts 15:2).

Once they got the doctrinal ducks in a row, it was time for them to move on. But their journey was a lot like those with siblings in the back seat of a vehicle.

Some time later Paul said to Barnabas, "Let us go back and visit the brothers in all the towns where we preached the word of the Lord and see how they are doing." Barnabas wanted to take John, also called Mark, with them, but Paul did not think it wise to take him, because he had deserted them in Pamphylia and had not continued with them in the work. They had such a sharp disagreement that they parted company. Barnabas took Mark and sailed for Cyprus, but Paul chose Silas and left, commended by the brothers to the grace of the Lord. He went through Syria and Cilicia, strengthening the churches (*Acts 15:36-41*).

This story isn't comfortable. The fact that two preachers disagreed so strongly that they couldn't stay together in ministry may stretch our understanding.

Fact is, most ministers are human. Just like regular people, some of them second-guess "Wet Paint" signs, have dandruff, and open sympathy notes placed under a windshield wiper by the police when their parking meter expires.

Sometimes ministers are expected to live perfect lives in an imperfect environment.

I heard of a pastor who tended to be a bit outspoken. Much of the time he should have left his mouth in *park* until his mind was in *drive*.

After a few rock-and-roll board meetings, the consensus among the esteemed members was that the Lord was probably "leading him to another field white unto harvest." Much to the delight of two in-law board members, the preacher suddenly announced he had taken a chaplaincy job at a local correctional facility.

A large crowd, including the board members and their extended families, came for his farewell service. With a semismirk, the pastor announced his new job and then announced his sermon text from John 14:2-3—"I go to prepare a place for you . . . that where I am, there ye may be also" (KJV).

Conflict—among clergy? What were they thinking? Who knows? But I'm glad the incident of Paul and Barnabas was included in the Bible. I think God wanted us to know that conflict can happen to any of us—and can be handled appropriately.

3. Conflict has a carbon imprint with frosting on it.

Like the little Nazarene boy who brought a casserole to school as a symbol of his faith for show and tell, church folks are known not only for what eats *at* them but also for what they *eat*. I have some friends who will probably order pizza at the Marriage Supper in heaven—and then wait around a million years for dessert.

Conflict has its own carbon imprint, with the frosting of personal or family characteristic on it. Tragically, conflict is an environmental problem: it always leaves smog in the air or litter on the sidewalks.

If it weren't for other people, we could get along with just about anyone.

The characteristic quirks of others do affect us. *Quirks* may even invade *qualities*, counteracting the best in a relationship and highlighting the worst.

At times we may not be able to reconcile Christian faith with a Christian's actions. Such was the case with Paul and his misgivings about the young disciple John Mark.

Paul was a Type A personality—the dominant, leader type. In his role as the apostle to the New Testament churches, he needed the attributes of decisiveness and action. For him, the rules of leadership were clearly laid out, and they did not include going AWOL.

The Scriptures are silent about the reasons John Mark left his Uncle Barnabas and his colleague, Paul. It might be one of those things we discuss with Brother John Mark while we're waiting for choir rehearsal in heaven.

Barnabas was probably a nurturer. He was the phlegmatic—the guy everyone loves who tries to be a peacemaker no matter how mad it makes everyone else. He was always the one to step in when others had walked out.

"Barnabas" was the nickname for a disciple named Joseph. Often there are adjectives that people silently—or loudly—tack on to a name, such as "Smart Aleck" Susie or "Big Mouth" Bob. Joseph was known as "Encourager" Barnabas—"Joseph, a Levite from Cyprus, whom the apostles called Barnabas (which means Son of Encouragement)" (Acts 4:36).

He was a cheerleader in the best sense of the word. Whether on the sidelines or in the stands, you could be sure that Barnabas would be "hollerin'" for you, as they might say in my native state of West Virginia. Barnabas always believed the best about others.

But Barnabas had a very "human" vein that coursed through him. Paul's take on the credentials of his nephew brought his teapot to a whistle. Obviously, he wasn't a pushover. He had taken sides with the underdog, John Mark, and wasn't about to walk away.

I know I could get into a theological smack-down over this, but I think there was a bit of holy stubbornness in him. It's the kind of stubbornness that stands for the right in the midst of the wrong, the kind Jesus showed when He overturned tables and threw out those who had set up a flea market in the Temple (see Matthew 21).

Conflict may have its positive side. Often when I travel overseas, I have to get the required shots. I'm always amused when the medical attendant gets ready to thrust that giant needle into the flesh of my skin and says, "This will be like a bee sting."

Don't get me wrong. I appreciate the consoling, but often I'm tempted to say, "And how many times have *you* been stung by a bee?" Some of those shots feel like the whole hive of bees had taken a ride in that syringe and wanted out at the next stop. But the sting had healing and preventive qualities.

Conflict has healing or preventive qualities. Adversity brings discovery. That pain in your side sent you to a doctor who discovered your appendicitis. That ankle that swelled up after you slid into third base sent you to the emergency room, where an X-ray discovered your hairline fracture. Conflicts can send us to the source—to the place where discovery is made that turns arguments into affirmations.

The disciples' disagreement ended in *discovery*, even though they hit a few speed bumps along the way.

John Mark might have been a sunny sanguine who started out with the enthusiasm of a contestant on "Let's Make a Deal" who had trouble with the finishing part. Maybe his youthful vision of mission work was clouded by bouts of seasickness from a few storms at sea or the rigors of ministry in a hostile environment. Somewhere along the way, he decided a boat ride home was his best option—and probably bought some Dramamine before the trip.

At Pamphylia, he packed his gym bag and left. And Paul never forgot it.

- Barnabas wanted to extend grace; Paul contended for the law.
- Barnabas stressed the importance of mercy; Paul emphasized the necessity of faithfulness.
- Barnabas desired to mentor his nephew; Paul thought John Mark didn't have the needed aptitude.

The discussion became a disagreement, and there was no easy solution. But conflicts can be solved in a Christlike and people-accepting way.

The solution: They doubled their ministry by splitting up the team. Barnabas took Mark and sailed for the island of Cyprus. Paul chose Silas and continued to Syria and Cilicia. That made two groups doing ministry. When conflict results in unresolved splinters, Satan is gratified. When conflict results in agreeable expansion, God is glorified.

Two opposing parties *can* reach a settlement. Tal Bonham tells of a convenience store in Louisiana that had strong chicory coffee brewing at all times.

One traveler said the owner of the store demanded that he drink a cup of coffee before driving on.

"No, thank you," said the customer. "I don't drink coffee."

This seemed to enrage the operator of the store, and he promptly pulled out a gun and held it on the customer and said, "I said, drink a cup of my coffee."

After the obliging traveler had drunk a cup of coffee, the store owner handed him the gun and said, "Now hold the gun on me while I drink a cup."[2]

4. Conflict is a curable as a cold.

Funny how medical science always frets about finding cures for the common cold. Guess they never met my granny. She had a simple formula: liniment plus cold equals cure. My mother updated the recipe by substituting Vicks VapoRub. It worked for me, but my brothers wore gas masks for a week. Sometimes the cure for anything, including conflict, is uncomfortable, but the gain is worth the pain.

Conflict resolution is a skill sadly lacking in the Church and in many homes. Too many times we think the godly response is to closet emotions and practice denial. This only compounds the problem.

When Christian people disagree, they should practice healthy boundaries for discussion and resolution.

1. Appeal for a chance to dialog.
2. Avoid hysteria, accusations, and slander.
3. Acknowledge the opposing viewpoint.
4. Affirm the pattern of Scripture (for relationships)—

   • **Charity in all things.** "Above all, love each other deeply, because love covers over a multitude of sins" (1 Peter 4:8).

   • **Peace if at all possible.** "If it is possible, as far as it depends on you, live at peace with everyone" (Romans 12:18).

   • **Unity as the end goal.** "Make every effort to keep the unity of the Spirit through the bond of peace" (Ephesians 4:3).

   • **Acceptance of the rights of others.** "Be devoted to one another in brotherly love. Honor one another above yourselves" (Romans 12:10).

   • **Agreement to move past the moment and build up God's work—either in unison or through an amicable parting of ways.** "Seek first his kingdom and his righteousness, and all these things will be given to you as well" (Matthew 6:33).

God's game plan is pretty simple:

As God's chosen people, holy and dearly loved, clothe yourselves with compassion, kindness, humility, gentleness and patience. Bear with each other and forgive whatever grievances you may have against one another. Forgive as the Lord forgave you. And over all these virtues put on love, which binds them all together in perfect unity (*Colossians 3:12-14*).

Building Bridges, Not Burning Fields

You remember the biblical story of Samson, the Nazarite with the build of a U-Haul truck, the looks of a J. C. Penney catalog model, and the hair of the "after" photo in a Rogaine commercial. Marrying the wrong woman for all the wrong reasons, he sought revenge on the enemy Philistines, who would use his wife to trick him into getting a haircut, stealing the secret of his strength. The outcomes of his conflicts usually weren't that pretty.

One time he outfoxed the enemy and became an animal control officer:

> Samson said to them, "This time I have a right to get even with the Philistines; I will really harm them." So he went out and caught three hundred foxes and tied them tail to tail in pairs. He then fastened a torch to every pair of tails, lit the torches and let the foxes loose in the standing grain of the Philistines. He burned up the shocks and standing grain, together with the vineyards and olive groves (*Judges 15:3-5*).

Intense conflict often ends in death—of some sort. In history, conflict has caused the bloody duels, the gory guillotine of the French Revolution, and the destruction of empires, notwithstanding the demise of the "fox brothers" and the back forty of the Philistines.

Maybe the outcome of your conflict won't have such a massive consequence. Maybe it won't mean physical death; but it may mean emotional or relational death—yours or theirs. The pain and sorrow will be equally devastating.

Divorce Court

In our culture the prevalence of divorce speaks to the power of conflict. According to a 2008 Barna Group study, among adults who have been married, one-third have experienced at least one divorce. That means that among all Americans eighteen years of age or older, whether they have been married or not, twenty-five percent have gone through a marital split.[3]

Are Christians immune to the mix? The same survey revealed that among Evangelical Christians, twenty-six percent have been divorced, as compared to a thirty-percent divorce rate among atheists and agnostics.[4]

Why the alarming stats? Someone has deliberately or inadvertently neglected another.

I've told the story of the busy executive who ran to the Mr. Coffee, his computer case trailing him in the breeze, quickly picked up his car keys, passed by his wife, blew her a kiss as he hurried to the car, and shouted back, "I love you terribly!"

Remembering that her husband had forgotten it was her birthday for the second year in a row, his wife shouted back, "You sure do!"

Neglect is nondenominational and nonsectarian. According to one online dictionary, the Latin root of the word "neglect" means to "disregard, ignore, or slight."[5] When marriage partners focus on personally achieving rather than corporately affirming, the result will always be a relationship deficit.

Stuff over "Real Stuff"

The lofty lure of the immediate has not only made its mark on our economy—it has made an ugly rip in the fabric of the home. In many cases the energy used in accumulating stuff has left married couples without even enough strength to wrap their arms around each other.

Conflict is usually caused by dueling interests. An unwillingness to deny self and put others first may be the prime catalyst behind conflict.

Behaviorist David J. Lieberman wrote, "Here's a general rule of thumb: If a person dislikes you without good reason, it's not because [he or] she doesn't like you, but because [he or] she doesn't like [himself or] herself very much. . . . Therefore you can turn a lion into a lamb by changing how [he or] she feels about [himself or] herself, which then changes how [he or] she feels about you." He offers a three-point insight about that person. The person—

- ***thinks you dislike [him or] her.*** You may have unintentionally not given [him or] her your full attention.
- ***feels threatened by you.*** You may remind [him or] her of what [he or] she wants but doesn't have.
- ***sees in you traits in [himself or] herself that [he or] she dislikes.*** You remind [him or] her of what [he or] she doesn't like about [himself or] herself.[6]

Of course, there's the ever-present conflict between good and evil, and such instances cannot be resolved except by the grace of God and the entrance of the light of Truth.

As God's children, we're called to consider the rights and opinions of others. "Each of you should look not only to your own interests, but also to the interests of others" (Philippians 2:4).

When you're committed to the Lordship of Christ, you're more able to resolve conflict because you're following the Great Commandment Jesus taught. "He answered: 'Love the Lord your God with all your heart and with all your soul and with all your strength and with all your mind'; and, 'Love your neighbor as yourself'" (Luke 10:27).

An administrative assistant was doing some water cooler bragging as the Memorial Day weekend approached: "We have a proud fighting tradition in my family! My great-great-great-great-great grandfather stood his ground at Bunker Hill. Then Great-grandfather valiantly joined up with the troops to destroy the Germans. My grandfather was at Pearl Harbor. And my father fought the North Koreans."

"Mercy!" one of her coworkers remarked. "Can't your family get along with anyone?"

Solutions R Us

I'm not a practicing counselor; but I've been practicing counseling for many years of ministry. Here are a few tips I've picked up during my leadership ministries.

How do you approach and solve conflict? Here are some key words that could factor in a solution.

"**Kindly.**" Trying to resolve a conflict by blunt confrontation is useless. The other party will simply try to defend his or her territory and self-esteem. Friendliness is next to godliness. And kindness will help pave the way to civil dialogue. "Get rid of all bitterness, rage, anger, harsh words, and slander, as well as all types of evil behavior. Instead, be kind to each other, tender-hearted, forgiving one another, just as God through Christ has forgiven you" (Ephesians 4:31-32).

"**Quickly.**" The longer you put off "that talk," the more it will simmer or boil on the stove. Jesus said, "Come to terms quickly with your enemy before it is too late and you are dragged into court, handed over to an officer, and thrown in jail" (Matthew 5:25, NLT). Take notice the warning "before it is too late." The situation could escalate.

"**Humbly.**" Taking your share of the blame for the conflict up front is a steady step toward a solution. In the same sermon, Jesus advised, "Listen to me! You can pray for anything, and if you believe, you will have it. But when you are praying, first forgive anyone you are holding a grudge against, so that your Father in heaven will forgive your sins, too" (Mark 11:24-25, NLT). When you put yourself in the position of being the judge, you must also remember that you were once the condemned. The Spirit of Christ is the Spirit of forgiveness—without dimensions.

"**Generously.**" Paul wrote, "Remember this—a farmer who plants only a few seeds will get a small crop. But the one who plants generously will get a generous crop" (2 Corinthians 9:6, NLT). Generosity fosters generosity. If your spirit is generous in the midst of a conflict, there's a good chance that generosity will be given in return—kindness for kindness, forgiveness for forgiveness.

Remember: nothing is greater than your mission, whether that mission is in your organization or in your home. Real relationships that are focused on the welfare of others and are Christlike and Spirit-driven are relationships that influence others for God and for good.

6

OF COURSE I'M LISTENING–
I JUST WASN'T PAYING
ATTENTION
Real Obedience

🐟 I called Bill Burch, my good friend in Phoenix, and told him that my sons and I were coming to Phoenix to watch our friend from Oklahoma City, Billy Bajema, play ball against the Arizona Cardinals. I said, "Bill, why don't you join us at the game?"

Bill said, "That would be great! I have two tickets, and I'll get two more."

Several calls and e-mails later, Seth, Adam, and I landed in Phoenix. I called my friend. "Bill, we've just landed in Phoenix. Let's plan to meet near the stadium and eat together."

At 4 P.M. I received a phone call from Bill, "Stan, I got us front-row seats!" Then there was a slight pause. "We *are* going to the Suns game, aren't we?"

Both of us had the latest in communications technology in our hands. Both of us had global positioning system products in our vehicles. Both of us had made hundreds of appointments in our lifetime.

Now there was just one problem: he had front-row tickets to a Phoenix Suns *basketball* game, and I was planning to attend a St. Louis Rams vs. Arizona Cardinals *football* game!

Premium seats, wrong sport!

Technology didn't help our communication. We said one thing, thought another, and heard something altogether different.

What we hear and how we respond are important not only in our relationships among our social network—they're also important, extremely so, in our relationship with God.

1. What you do relates to *whose* you are.

The framework of the Christian faith is built over the foundation of personal spiritual obedience. "For in the gospel a righteousness from God is revealed, a righteousness that is by faith from first to last, just as it is written: 'The righteous will live by faith'" (Romans 1:17).

Smartphones are wonderful—except when they *aren't* wonderful!

When the Toler brothers were preteens, we couldn't have imagined owning handheld phones that would talk to us even before we made a call. In fact, when we were preteens, telephones had a whole other life of their own. We learned more about the neighbors by accident than we would ever know on purpose. Telephones used to be on party lines, meaning more than one family was on the same line. When you heard that one of the folks down the road had gone to the doctor, you would hear the diagnosis on the party line before they even got a chance to tell their kids!

Now with handheld smartphones and voice recognition, you can enter a number without boxing with all those little keypad thingies. Just hit a button, and you'll hear "Say a command." You just talk at the phone and say something like "Call pharmacy." Sooner than you can stifle a sneeze, there will be someone from the pharmacy who will answer and then stand by a computer keyboard, type in a remedy, wait for your visit, and then whistle "Happy Days Are Here Again" while you walk up to the counter to make your purchase.

God's command of obedience identifies Him as owner. The one whose commands we keep is the one who possesses our allegiance, our love, and our devotion. In fact, the whole purpose of Christ's coming to earth was to empower us to obey God, to live in "holiness and righteousness before him all our days" (Luke 1:75).

**Obedience without appropriate action
is not real obedience.**

David McKenna reflected on the life of Wesley:

John Wesley lived in the time between the dying age of agriculture and the dawning age of industry. No transition in human history is more difficult than the time between ages, and human beings are dragged into the future kicking and screaming. Consider the eighteenth-century farmer in England who saw his first steam engine huffing and puffing along a railroad track. He took one look and said, "There has to be a horse in there someplace![1]

All the huffing and puffing of that steam engine was useless without the motivating factor. It's the same for your journey. Jesus said "If you love me, you will obey what I command" (John 14:15).

You've seen it a hundred times or more: a crisply uniformed line of soldiers stands at attention before their country's colors and waits for the next word from the commanding officer:

"Eyes *left*!"

"Present *arms*!"

"Forward *march*!"

The next actions of each soldier will determine whether he or she will take his or her seat in the mess hall that evening or have a staring match with the ground while doing a hundred pushups. Obedience without appropriate action is not real obedience. The wisdom writer closed his book with this final word: "Fear God. Do what he tells you" (Ecclesiastes 12:13, TM). In other words, respect deserves an appropriate reaction.

Under the Old Covenant, obedience was more than a proof of love—it was necessary to life. Check it out for yourself:

- Priests were struck down in the Temple if they didn't keep the order of service.
- Disobey Moses' commands, and a sinkhole could instantly swallow you up.
- Walk too close to the cart carrying the ark of the covenant, and you could suffer cardiac arrest.

There wasn't much wiggle room in Old Testament times.

Thankfully, Jesus paid the membership dues for those living in New Testament times and forward. Follow Him by faith, live under the covenant of His grace, obey the principles of His Word—the Bible—and the looming cloud of ceremonial constraints is lifted. "The law was given through Moses; grace and truth came through Jesus Christ" (John 1:17).

The machinery of spiritual obedience is already in place—and the manual has already been written. You are in the front line with those soldiers, waiting for a command and willing to respond. If your heart is in tune with the Commander, you'll make a five-star difference in your relationship.

I heard of two elderly gentlemen who were sitting on the patio of an assisted living complex. One of the gentlemen said, "You know, Fred, I've had my eye on one of those ladies who come to our chapel service every week—the one who plays the piano. She looks sixty-ish."

Fred didn't look up from the Medicaid manual he got from the government. "Saw her myself last week, even with my eyesight the way it is. *Very* attractive."

Sam didn't like the way Fred said *very.* "Now get that out of your mind—or whatever's left of it. I saw her first! And besides that, I'm thinking about asking her to go with me to the shuffleboard playoffs!"

There was a minute or so of silence. Once Sam got it under control, he continued. "You know, Fred, I'm only in my early eighties, and if weren't for this arthritis, I'd look a lot younger. Do you suppose I'd stand a better chance of taking her to the playoffs if I told her I was in my seventies?"

Fred kept reading for prescription tips in the manual. "Sam, she probably knows you made a fortune selling them exhaust pipes. Think you'd stand a better chance if you told her you were in your late nineties and only one aorta short of a good heart."

Grace doesn't overlook dishonesty or disobedience—it's there as a remedy. Jehovah gave Moses the Ten Commandments, written on tablets of stone. These were the standard, the sledgehammer of obedience. But God promised that under the new covenant He would write His laws upon the hearts of His people—they would have an inner compulsion and willing spirit for obedience:

> This is the covenant I will make with the house of Israel after that time, declares the Lord. I will put my laws in their minds and write them on their hearts. I will be their God, and they will be my people (*Hebrews 8:10*).

2. What you hear relates to who you are.

You've heard the expression "Blood is thicker than water." That means that if two promotions are scheduled for your shop and the boss's daughter just started working there after completing her MBA, you'd better not put a down payment on new kitchen cabinets. Daughter stands a pretty good chance of a pay raise.

When you read the Old Testament book of 1 Samuel, you'll see that the sons of Eli, the priest in the Temple, were promoted to assist him but didn't share enough common sense to light a candle with a blow torch, and their hearts were as dry as the pumpkin seeds in last year's jack-o-lantern.

They shut down their line of communication with Jehovah God and even made a mockery of the Temple ceremonies (see 1 Samuel 2:12-17.) The custom was for the priests to eat from whatever was on a fork after it was plunged into the kettle of boiling meat during the sacrifice. Eli's sons were taking the sacrificial meat from the Israelites before they had a chance to offer it properly.

In so many words, they said the priest preferred steak tartare. Now, for those of you who don't have that on your food chart, "tartare" means uncooked meat. Raw! As in "Just wave that hamburger patty over the barbecue, Mabel."

Eli's sons, Hophni and Phinehas, later suffered for their shortcuts. But theirs is a lesson to learn. Do what God tells you to do—for the sake of your relationship with Him and with others.

- He might be telling you to have an accountability partner check your Internet searches.
- He might be telling you to stay away from that "iffy" friendship you know could turn into an immoral relationship.
- He might be telling you to spend some time outdoors rather than trolling the discount store aisles for another gadget that you won't use six months later anyway.
- He might be telling you not to bypass that meeting with your supervisor or another colleague to discuss your wrong attitude.

• He might be telling you to read a book rather than watch a video.

Whatever He might be telling you, you can be sure that it beats Satan's alternative. "'I know the plans I have for you,' says the LORD. 'They are plans for good and not for disaster, to give you a future and a hope'" (Jeremiah 29:11, NLT).

I Think I Hear Someone Listening

God once again intervened in the treatment of His people. It all began in the heart of a consecrated woman who was childless. Her name was Hannah, the second wife (customary in Old Testament times) of a man named Elkanah. His other wife, Pinnanah, had children and mocked Hannah's inability to conceive. But God was listening.

In bitterness of soul Hannah wept much and prayed to the Lord. And she made a vow, saying, "O Lord Almighty, if you will only look upon your servant's misery and remember me, and not forget your servant but give her a son, then I will give him to the Lord for all the days of his life, and no razor will ever be used on his head." As she kept on praying to the LORD, Eli observed her mouth. Hannah was praying in her heart, and her lips were moving but her voice was not heard. Eli thought she was drunk and said to her, "How long will you keep on getting drunk? Get rid of your wine." "Not so, my lord," Hannah replied, "I am a woman who is deeply troubled. I have not been drinking wine or beer; I was pouring out my soul to the LORD. Do not take your servant for a wicked woman; I have been praying here out of my great anguish and grief." Eli answered, "Go in peace, and may the God of Israel grant you what you have asked of him" (1 Samuel 1:10-17).

The scene is almost too personal to view. But throughout time, the obedience of one has resulted in the rescue of another—especially in the case of our Lord. "In bringing many sons to glory, it was fitting that God, for whom and through whom everything exists, should make the author of their salvation perfect through suffering" (Hebrews 2:10. See also Hebrews 11.)

The answer to Hannah's prayer was a son, whom she named Samuel. And, as promised, she gave her son in service to God.

The boy Samuel ministered before the LORD under Eli. In those days the word of the LORD was rare; there were not many visions.

One night Eli, whose eyes were becoming so weak that he could barely see, was lying down in his usual place. The lamp of God had not yet gone out, and Samuel was lying down in the temple of the LORD, where the ark of God was. Then the Lord called Samuel.

Samuel answered, "Here I am." And he ran to Eli and said, "Here I am; you called me."

But Eli said, "I did not call; go back and lie down." So he went and lay down.

Again the LORD called, "Samuel!" And Samuel got up and went to Eli and said, "Here I am; you called me."

"My son," Eli said, "I did not call; go back and lie down."

Now Samuel did not yet know the LORD: The word of the LORD had not yet been revealed to him (*1 Samuel 3:1-7*).

A little boy in school was corrected by his teacher for staring through a window during class. Several times the teacher called out his name, but there was no response. Frustrated, the teacher said loudly, "Joshua McKenzie! Are you hard of hearing?"

Josh answered just loud enough for the teacher to hear, "No, sir. I'm not hard of hearing—I'm *hard of listening.*"

Samuel wasn't "hard of listening."

The LORD called Samuel a third time, and Samuel got up and went to Eli and said, "Here I am; you called me."

Then Eli realized that the LORD was calling the boy. So Eli told Samuel, "Go and lie down, and if he calls you, say, 'Speak, LORD, for your servant is listening.'" So Samuel went and lay down in his place.

The LORD came and stood there, calling as at the other times, "Saumuel! Samuel!"

The Samuel said, "Speak, for your servant is listening" (*1 Samuel 3:8-10*).

Samuel got the message. He heard loud and clear.

Almost every day you can find an ad in the newspaper or on web sites for a free hearing test. I have a friend who says that the only free thing about all of that is reading *People* magazine in the waiting room. After leaving the doctor's office with a hearing aid that cost more than his first car, Jerry said, "The deficit in my hearing was gone, but now there was a recession in my checkbook."

How about you? Have you had a "listening test" lately? Here's one:

- Pick a quiet time, in the midst of or away from the busiest part of the day.
- Go to a quiet place—somewhere you can focus your attention.
- Open your Bible to the beginning chapters of the Psalms.
- Start scanning the chapters until a word or phrase stands out.
- Read that chapter one verse at a time and one phrase at a time when you get to a standout verse.
- Let the verse—or word or phrase—fill your thoughts.
- Say *yes* to whatever the Holy Spirit applies from that focal point, and talk to Him about what He wants to teach you from it.
- Quiet your heart as you reflect on the truth.

I know that if I don't begin my day listening to my Heavenly Father, I won't be as sharp in my listening to *others*. Reading

God's Word and talking to Him in prayer is a habit I never want to break.

In his book *The Divine Mentor,* Wayne Cordeiro illustrates the importance of practice.

Ignace Jan Paderewski was a renowned Polish pianist who lived in the first half of the twentieth century. When his government requested that he play concerts in order to raise money, Paderewski, a patriot and a willing citizen, replied, "I will be a part of the war effort under one condition. You must allow me every day to continue playing scales, three hours a day. Pay me for eight hours; but I will play scales for three."[2]

Samuel practiced his listening. It's good discipline for all of life. Mother Teresa said, "God speaks in the silence of the heart. Listening is the beginning of prayer."[3]

To talk or not to talk—that is the answer.

I've noticed that people who listen have even deeper relationships than those who spend all their time talking. People need not only a shoulder to cry on—they need an ear to talk into. Listening may be one of the most important things we can do for others. And someone who has learned how to listen to God is one who will have a greater sensitivity in listening to others.

**Someone who has learned how to listen to God
is one who will have a greater sensitivity
in listening to others.**

Of course, there's a time for talking to other people in a relationship as well—long talks, talks that open the soul and courageously let its most treasured thoughts take flight, short talks that simply affirm others:

"I love you."

"Thank you."

"I appreciate you."

"I'm sorry."

I heard of a man who almost had a heart attack when he was offered free food on an airline flight. The flight attendant asked the magic question in one word, "Lunch?"

Thinking he would take advantage of this rare occasion in a time when airlines are known for their cutbacks as much as they are for their takeoffs, the traveler replied rather smugly, "And what might our choices be today?"

The attendant's answer was just as brief and to-the-point as her original question: "Yes or no."

Maybe one of the reasons we need to work on our listening to God is because we also need to work on our *talking* to God. For many, prayer time is either pre-snack or a pre-sleep. Sometimes they even get their "God-is-greats" mixed up with their "Now-I-lay-me-down-to-sleeps," and it may come out sounding something like "Great! God is *asleep!*"

He's not asleep, you know. "Indeed, he who watches over Israel never tires and never sleeps" (Psalm 121:4, NLT).

Wow! A wide-awake God! That should help you sleep at night.

3. What you become depends on what you do with who you are.

In his book *What Matters Most*, Hyrum Smith quoted from the autobiography of Nelson Mandela:

> When I walked out of prison, that was my mission, to liberate the oppressed and the oppressor both. Some say that has now been achieved. But I know that that is not the case. The truth is that we are not yet free; we have merely achieved the freedom to be free, the right not to be op-

pressed. We have not taken the final step of our journey, but the first step on a longer and even more difficult road.[4] I'm sure Samuel's experience was a bit unnerving. He was young; he was alone in the Temple—probably without a fluorescent nightlight—and he wasn't trained to listen for God's voice. But he reacted in a way that would please his momma. "The LORD came and called as before, 'Samuel! Samuel!' And Samuel replied, 'Speak, your servant is listening'" (1 Samuel 3:10).

God not only called Samuel—He also gave him the game plan he would use in serving Israel as a prophet and judge.

As Samuel grew up, the LORD was with him, and everything Samuel said was wise and helpful. And all the people of Israel from one end of the land to the other knew that Samuel was confirmed as a prophet of the LORD. The LORD continued to appear at Shiloh and gave messages to Samuel there at the Tabernacle (*1 Samuel 3:19-21*, NLT).

Now Samuel was free from the immediate confusion (he wasn't hearing voices anymore), but he had just started a longer and even more difficult road.

Samuel responded to God's in three important ways:

• *He listened.* Notice where Samuel was sleeping when he heard the voice of God—"in the Tabernacle near the Ark of God" (1 Samuel 3:3, NLT). The Ark of the Covenant was the symbol that represented the very presence of the Lord. Naturally, the closer you get to someone the easier it is to hear what he or she says, and subsequently to do what he or she asks. Andrew Murray said, "God is ready to assume full responsibility for the life wholly yielded to Him."[5]

• *He reflected.* Samuel was able to tell Eli what had happened verbatim. "Samuel told Eli everything; he didn't hold anything back" (verse 18, NLT). Mark Twain said in his autobiography, "When I was younger, I could remember anything, whether it had happened or not; but my faculties are decaying now and soon I shall be so old I cannot remember any but the things that never happened." Most of us have trouble remembering the things that happened, let alone trying to remember the things that didn't. Not Samuel—he remembered everything, because the Holy Spirit sealed it in his heart. Jesus promised, "When he, the Spirit of truth, comes, he will guide you into all truth. He will not speak on his own; he will speak only what he hears, and he will tell you what is yet to come. He will bring glory to me by taking from what is mine and making it known to you. All that belongs to the Father is mine. That is why I said the Spirit will take from what is mine and make it known to you" (*John 16:13-15*).

- **He acted.** "As Samuel grew up, the Lord was with him, and everything Samuel said proved to be reliable. And all Israel, from Dan in the north to Beersheba in the south, knew that Samuel was confirmed as a prophet of the Lord" (1 Samuel 3:19-20). The best kind of listening is the kind that responds in a reflective and responsible way—in a way that brings affirmation to others. Samuel's listening and obedience endeared him as a man of God and a prophet of truth to the people of Israel.

Author Calvin Miller wrote about Elizabeth of Hungary, a devoted saint of the thirteenth century. He writes about her intense love for and marriage to Louis IV. So deep was her love, Miller writes, that she would weep in his presence. When Louis IV was killed in the Crusades, Elizabeth grieved—and then grew in her love for Christ. "The glory of God settled on her life," He says. "Her passion for Christ and her addiction to the glory of God brought the mystery of godliness and her uncontained love together. Wherever these things meet, Jesus walks again upon the earth. Pentecost is reborn. Obedience is the watchword. Worship is the mystique. God waits for those who will love Him and who hunger for things too excellent to be understood."[6]

Will you be obedient? Settle then three things:

1. The position issue: Who will be first in my life?
2. The permission issue: Who has control of my life?
3. The possession issue: Who owns my stuff?

Godspeed to you in your exciting journey of faith and obedience.

7

WHEN THERE ARE TOO MANY
HANDS IN THE COOKIE JAR
Real Restoration

🎬 A noted late-night comedian addressed the camera to apologize for being caught in a pattern of affairs with production staff members of his television show. Saying how sorry he was that he had caused them to be harassed by news media, he admitted that his live-in lover of over two decades, and now his legal wife, had also been hurt by the revelations.

His final word on the subject—at least for the night—was to admit that it would be tough work to patch things up with the missus: "Let me tell you, folks—I got my work cut out for me."

The studio audience reaction was a mix of laughs and applause to his admissions and the subplot jokes he inserted during his explanation.

Afterward, reporters interviewed audience members outside the theater where his show is taped. One reaction was sadly characteristic: "He's only human—and he's still a great entertainer."

The comedian had joined a long list of politicians, business tycoons, and sports figures—the subjects of the comedian's jokes in the past—who had been collectively caught with their hands in the cookie jar and had brought disastrous consequences to themselves and to their social network.

R. Albert Mohler Jr., president of the Southern Baptist Theological Seminary, asked a very pertinent question in a *Christian Post* online column: "Are art and artists above moral accountability?" The answer was imbedded in the same quote, "The Hollywood elite seem to believe so—and even to be willing to lend their names to the defense of the morally indefensible."[1]

However, that question was first answered in the Scriptures: "Those who sin are opposed to the law of God, for all sin opposes the law of God" (1 John 3:4, NLT).

No matter what kind of legal representation they may have, there is no "sin exemption" that can be written into the contract of a celebrity—or anyone else.

Santa Clauses

It's funny to me how some contract clauses turn into "Santa Clauses"—they're all dressed up, promise lots of goodies, but are just as fabled as the yearly intercontinental ride in a reindeer sled. Some of my "celebrity" friends have been forgotten at the airport, locked out of their own hotel rooms, served butter sandwiches, and have been assigned something akin to a janitor's closet as a dressing room!

I guess they needed a good lawyer—just like the pastor who made the mistake of asking the wrong question in a junior high boys' Sunday School class: "Eddie, do you know who knocked down the walls of Jericho?"

Slumped in his steel folding chair, the boy suddenly straightened up and pointed an index finger. "Don't go tryin' to pin that on me, Preacher. I wasn't anywhere near that wall."

Things got worse at the Golden Corral restaurant after church. "Mom," the boy said, "the preacher accused me of breaking some wall—in front of the whole Sunday School class! I was humiliated!"

Monday morning, early, the young pastor received a call. "Good morning, Pastor," the voice sweetly announced. After the customary "How are you?" the caller's tone changed.

"Now, Pastor, you know I'm not one to cause any trouble."

The pastor didn't answer.

"But Charles said you made an accusation about him during Sunday School yesterday. Something about him vandalizing church property, I think it was."

A big groggy at 6:00 A.M. on his day off, the pastor said, "I'm sorry, Mrs. Friedendork, but I don't remember saying anything like that."

After a bit of chit-chat about the "wall" incident, the caller signed off. "Well, Pastor, I hope you have a good day off. I won't bother you anymore today; I'll just discuss this with my husband—and perhaps some other members of the church board."

The pastor hung up the phone and sat back down at the breakfast table. "Who was that?" the pastor's wife asked.

"Mrs. Freidendork," he replied.

Fear widened his wife's eyes. "What did *she* want?"

The pastor took a spoonful of All-Bran. "She just called to tell me about some 'wars and rumors of wars.'"

At the Tuesday night board meeting, one of the members asked if he could say a word.

"Pastor, it has come to our attention that the Friedendork boy was publicly accused of damaging a wall in the Jericho Youth Center.

"Now, Reverend, the Freidendorks are charter members of the church and give that $500 in tithe every year. Why don't we just put that matter behind us, take some money out of the building management fund, and repair the damages?"

Too bad the pastor didn't have a "Jericho wall" clause in his contract.

King David needed a *morality* clause in his contract with Israel.

The shepherd turned sovereign had a major blip on the radar screen of his life: He took a day off from fighting and made a *sighting* that would forever change his life.

As a result of being caught with his hand in the cookie jar, he suffered severe emotional, spiritual, relational, and physical trauma.

⟨◈⟩⟨◈⟩⟨◈⟩

Failure rarely announces itself. It slips through the side door of life and catches us by surprise, like a thief in the night.

Failure in any area of life rarely announces itself. It slips through the side door and catches us by surprise, like a thief in the night. No one prepares refreshments for its arrival.

- No newlywed expects divorce proceedings.
- No parent expects to raise a rebel child.
- No middle-aged couple expects an affair.
- No friendship expects conflict.
- No employee expects accusations.
- No executive expects a publicized bankruptcy.

Failure has long been a problem for the human family. But failure is simply a blessing that has been turned into a *burden* because of someone's personal sin. Many of the things God intended for our good are used for the wrong reasons.

For example, sexuality was created by a wise and loving God, but its misuse becomes a tool of carnal self-centeredness. From ancient times, including Bible times, people have been burdened with sexual sin and dysfunction.

An illicit flirtation that turns into planned fornication is too common. Many themes for media producers are based on sexual indiscretion, some even including children.

Lust is often the subject of laughter, but those caught in its trap don't get the joke—they get only emotional pain, contagious diseases, and eventual rejection.

According to a contemporary country song titled "Reasons I Cheat," if life's getting a little too tough for you, or your marriage is requiring you to take a little responsibility, or you just feel that you're over the hill and need a new thrill—it's okay to cheat—at least according to this tired song.

Songs and singers come in all shapes, sizes, and aptitude. A group of music teachers discussed some of the strangest answers they had received to their test questions.

I'm a collector of "top ten" lists. Here are some favorite teacher questions and student answers that have to do with music—tired country songs or otherwise.

10. Q: What is a virtuoso? A: Virtuoso is a musician with really high morals.

9. Q: Who is Henry Purcell? A: Henry Purcell is a well-known composer few people have ever heard of.

8. Q: What is it called when two people sing together? A: When two people sing together, it's called a duel.

7. Q: What are kettle drums called? A: Kettle drums.

6. Q: What is your favorite lullaby? A: My favorite lullaby is the "Bronze" Lullaby.

5. Q: What is a harp? A: A harp is a piano without any clothes on.

4. Q: What is a refrain? A: "Refrain" means "Don't do it."

3. Q: What do most authorities say about the music of antiquity? A: Most authorities say that music of antiquity was written long ago.

2. Q: What is "Agnes Dei"? A: Agnes Dei is a woman who sings in church.

1. Q: When did Beethoven die? A: Beethoven expired in 1827 and later died from this.[2]

I guess people do get their music matters mixed up.

And speaking of mixed-up music matters, the trouble with such songs as "Reasons I Cheat" is that they are so terribly out of tune—no matter in what key they're sung. There really is no valid reason to cheat. Broken hearts lay at the roadside of those who have taken that route.

Not all broken relationships are the result of moral failure, but many are. Let's examine the process of moral failure in the life of King David—and the subsequent steps to restoration. We can see it in several steps.

The Path of Indiscretion

There's no social or spiritual height so secure that it can keep anyone from taking a tumble. David was chosen by God's nation, anointed by God's prophet, yet he experienced one of the most celebrated moral failures in history. Author Og Mandino said, "I will not allow yesterday's success to lull me into today's complacency, for this is the great foundation of failure."[3]

But it didn't happen all at once. There were some slow-motion steps in his fall, seen in the Old Testament book of 2 Samuel.

Idleness

In the spring, at the time when kings go off to war, David sent Joab out with the king's men and the whole Israelite army. They destroyed the Ammonites and besieged Rabbah. But David remained in Jerusalem (*2 Samuel 11:1*).

At this point David wasn't doing anything wrong; he just wasn't doing what he was supposed to be doing. His place was on the battlefront, but he chose to stay at home. I think there's a principle that could be used in almost any environment: If you choose to do *nothing* when you're supposed to be doing *something*, you open yourself to *anything.*

Jesus made it very clear: a vacant room can easily be turned into a workshop for the devil.

When a corrupting spirit is expelled from someone, it drifts along through the desert looking for an oasis, some unsuspecting soul it can bedevil. When it doesn't find anyone, it says, "I'll go back to my old haunt." On return, it finds the person swept and dusted, but vacant. It then runs out and rounds up seven other spirits dirtier than itself and they all move in, whooping it up. That person ends up far worse than if he'd never gotten cleaned up in the first place (*Luke 11:24-26, TM*).

**If you choose to do *nothing* when
you're supposed to be doing *something*,
you open yourself to *anything.***

Guard your idle moments.
- When you use the quiet time in your office or in your home for surfing the Web indiscriminately instead of purposefully, you might be preparing a room for the devil's workshop.
- When you choose to be idle instead of "being about my Father's business" (like Jesus), you open yourself to misdirection and often wrong affiliations.

Of course, you need downtime, but it should be just as prayerfully planned as your busy time. The caution is in letting your downtime *become* your busy time.

Lust

"One evening David got up from his bed and walked around on the roof of the palace. From the roof he saw a woman bathing. The woman was very beautiful" (2 Samuel 11:2).

- There wasn't anything wrong with the *walk*—exercise is good for you.
- There wasn't anything wrong with the *look*—that was a normal reaction, factory-installed.
- The wrong was in the *contemplation*—"*very* beautiful." The *saw* turned to *sin* because he stored the "photo capture" on the hard drive of his heart. James cautioned, "Each one is tempted when, by his own evil desire, he is dragged away and enticed. Then, after desire has conceived, it gives birth to sin; and sin, when it is full-grown, gives birth to death" (James 1:14-15).

The world seems to be in love with lust. It advertises it, tapes it, and plays it over and over on monitor screens or on the Internet. But God hates it. It's in the list of the top seven things He detests (see Proverbs 6:16-19). Proverbs 6:18 says the Lord hates "a heart that devises wicked schemes, feet that are quick to rush into evil."

David didn't wake up that morning and say to himself, *Today I'm going to devise a wicked scheme.* He just became a victim to that tiny hole in his soul—that empty place that had been swept clean and not filled with good things (see Philippians 4:8).

Who knows? Maybe David needed someone or something to bolster his image or his courage.

Listen to the words of a man who ended up with a ruined marriage and a ruined career after a one-night stand: "Adultery isn't something that happens with the act—it happens months beforehand. It's an attitude. You disconnect yourself from the person you've said you're spending the rest of your life with."

Sin

James rightly said, "After desire has conceived, it gives birth to sin."

> David sent someone to find out about her. The man said, "Isn't this Bathsheba, the daughter of Eliam and the wife of Uriah the Hittite?" Then David sent messengers to get her. She came to him, and he slept with her. (She had purified herself from her uncleanness.) Then she went back home (2 Samuel 11:3-4).

The world often sees adultery as a "victimless crime." Online law commentator Richard S. Frase wrote,

> In the continuing debate over the proper scope of the criminal law, it has frequently been suggested that certain crimes are in reality "victimless" and that all statutes defining such offenses should be repealed or at least substantially restricted (Schur; Packer; Morris and Hawkins). Although all authors do not use the term in the same way, the following offenses have been included in the victimless crime category: public drunkenness; vagrancy; various sexual acts usually involving consenting adults (fornication, adultery, bigamy, incest, sodomy, homosexuality, and prostitution).[4]

One author even wrote a book entitled *Affair! How to Manage Every Aspect of Your Extramarital Relationship with Passion, Discretion, and Dignity*. The publisher described it as "a thoughtful, detailed discussion of every aspect of considering, preparing for, beginning, and conducting a successful and emotionally fulfilling extramarital affair."[5]

But the seventh commandment puts that book on another shelf; it says, "You shall not commit adultery" (Exodus 20:14). Adultery is sin—breaking God's law on purpose—and it isn't a victimless crime: the sinless Son of God, Jesus Christ, was killed to pay its penalty.

**Sin has you only when you take a first step
in its direction—and keep walking!**

David's sighting turned to an evil strategy session—because he purposefully put that session on his calendar. Sin has you only when you take a first step in its direction—and keep walking!

Deceit

Sin always multiplies. Try as you may to control its population, it will birth an offspring. The king, who never dreamed he would break the seventh commandment by committing adultery, is suddenly faced with breaking the sixth by committing murder. It is almost as if he was involved in a carnal countdown. See it again:

- He started with breaking the *tenth*—"You shall not covet."
- Then he broke the *seventh*—"You shall not commit adultery."
- And then ended up breaking the *sixth*—"You shall not murder."
- Where was he headed? He was headed for the top, in reverse order, toward the *first*—"You shall have no other gods before me."

But because of his problems with the first commandment, making other gods in his life, he ended up breaking the rest. It is standard operating procedure: When God isn't first in your life, everything else begins to unravel (see 2 Samuel 11).

The woman conceived and sent word to David, saying, "I am pregnant" (verse 5).

So David sent this word to Joab: "Send me Uriah the Hittite." And Joab sent him to David (verse 6).

In the morning David wrote a letter to Joab and sent it with Uriah (verse 11).

So while Joab had the city under siege, he put Uriah at a place where he knew the strongest defenders were (verse 16).

When the men of the city came out and fought against Joab, some of the men in David's army fell; moreover, Uriah the Hittite died (verse 17).

To be sure, not all the consequences of failure happen in the first round. Other things begin to crowd the arena, like reporters in a championship boxing event after a judge's decision is made.

Distrust

Once the epitome of leadership, David now was dealing with sin that took him off the Fortune 500 "A list." He began to develop a Wall-Street-sized sham:

Joab sent David a full account of the battle. He instructed the messenger: "When you have finished giving the king this account of the battle, the king's anger may flare up, and he may ask you, 'Why did you get so close to the city to fight? Didn't you know they would shoot arrows from the wall? Who killed Abimelech son of Jerub-Besheth? Didn't a woman throw an upper millstone on him from the wall, so that he died in Thebez? Why did you get so close to the wall?' If he asks you this, then say to him, 'Also, your servant Uriah the Hittite is dead'" (*2 Samuel 11:18-21*).

Setbacks

You'll never go forward as long as your back is turned to the right. Faith is a forward motion. You see it in the Scriptures. For example, the apostle Paul was always heading in the direction of the goal line—*toward* the prize of the high calling of God in Christ Jesus.

The messenger set out, and when he arrived he told David everything Joab had sent him to say. The messenger said to David, "The men overpowered us and came out against us in the open, but we drove them back to the entrance to the city gate. Then the archers shot arrows at your servants from the wall, and some of the king's men died. Moreover, your servant Uriah the Hittite is dead" (*2 Samuel 11:22-24*). Character was beginning to crumble. Now lying was in the mix.

Reversal of Fortune

David told the messenger, "Say this to Joab: 'Don't let this upset you; the sword devours one as well as another. Press the attack against the city and destroy it.' Say this to encourage Joab" (*2 Samuel 11:25*).

Joab, David's commanding officer, was caught in David's trap, and the enemy's threats were obviously giving Joab anxiety attacks.

Until a relationship conflict is settled, reversal of fortune—relational or otherwise—is always waiting on deck.

Extended Pain

"When Uriah's wife heard that her husband was dead, she mourned for him" (2 Samuel 11:26). Indiscretion brought injury! It always does. Everyone knows that at the outset—they just cover it up with rationalization.

Unresolved conflict also has a ninety-nine-point-nine-percent chance of causing pain. It may be hidden, but it will linger and increase by the day.

The Healing from Indiscretion

I heard of a little boy who listened to the African-American spiritual "There Is a Balm in Gilead" and asked his mom why people in church were singing about folks on his favorite show *Gilligan's Island*: "There is a bomb in Gilligan's head."

Actually the song has a very meaningful message. It answers the question of Jeremiah, the weeping prophet, over the creeping spiritual and political decay of Israel. "Is there no balm in

Gilead? Is there no physician there? Why then is there no healing for the wound of my people?" (Jeremiah 8:22).

Throughout modern history, the answer in the beloved
spiritual has echoed in song, brush arbors, camp meetings,
church sanctuaries, auditoriums, or around campfires,

There is a balm in Gilead to make the wounded whole;

There is a balm in Gilead to heal the sin-sick soul.

The healing ointment of the Great Physician, Jesus Christ,
is sufficient for anyone—and anything.

I like the New Testament story of the lame man whom Jesus healed by the pool of Bethesda: "Instantly, the man was
healed! He rolled up the mat and began walking! But this mir-
acle happened on the Sabbath day. So the Jewish leaders ob-
jected. They said to the man who was cured, 'You can't work
on the Sabbath! It's illegal to carry that sleeping mat!'" (John
5:9-10, NLT).

The rules of the Pharisees were so strict that they considered rolling up and carrying a mat on the Sabbath as work.

They didn't stop with the healed man however; they sought
out Jesus for being an accomplice. "So the Jewish leaders began
harassing Jesus for breaking the Sabbath rules. But Jesus replied, 'My Father never stops working, so why should I?" (John
5:16-17, NLT).

Did you get that? The Physician is *always* on call. And the
remedy is always in stock.

Both routes on the path of healing—the one going down
and the one coming back—are covered by the love, grace, wisdom, salvation, and sanctification made possible by the sacrificial death and triumphant resurrection of the Christ.

The prophet saw it through Spirit-anointed eyes. "It was our
weaknesses he carried. . . . But he was wounded and crushed
for our sins. He was beaten that we might have peace. He was
whipped, and we were healed!" (Isaiah 53:4-5, NLT).

❧❧❧

Both routes on the path of healing—the one
going down and the one coming back—are
covered by the love, grace, wisdom, salvation, and
sanctification made possible by the sacrificial death
and triumphant resurrection of the Christ.

What's the process? How do you get from where you are to
where you need to be spiritually? Follow David on his way back
from the brink. The "route" is given in the historical writing
of the Psalms—penned by David himself (see Psalm 51). The
NIV version of Psalm 51 includes this subtitle: "For the director
of music. A psalm of David. When the prophet Nathan came
to him after David had committed adultery with Bathsheba."

The path of your conflict may not be a moral indiscretion.
But conflict is conflict, and healing is healing; so let's apply the
process.

Step One: Admission

In 2 Samuel 12 the wise prophet Nathan told a story about
a rich man who had plenty of sheep yet stole a favorite sheep
of a poor man. Of course, the story was aimed at the king who
stole Bathsheba, the wife of the poor soldier, Uriah.

The story hit the target over David's heart: "Have mercy on
me, O God, according to your unfailing love; according to your
great compassion blot out my transgressions" (Psalm 51:1).

In David's case the failure was pretty obvious. In other conflict situations it may not be so cut and dried. But the first step
is still applicable: Admit your part. No excuses—just admit
your part of the wrong.

Step Two: Repentance

"Wash away all my iniquity and cleanse me from my sin"
(Psalm 51:2).

As Christians, we long for a life of holiness, allowing the Lord to conform our hearts to his perfect will and to His likeness. A prayer we might pray is *Lord, I give you anything and everything that would keep me from putting you first in my life, no matter the personal cost.* Once David saw the depths of his sin next to the heights of God's holiness, he felt lower than antlers on a centipede.

True repentance is all or nothing. It's an *I'm sorry*
that runs deep to the soul, deep enough to admit
its need and abandon any previous plans for the
sake of God's restoration.

I was a barber during my college days. Often a customer would say, "Just take a little off the top." One look at the creeping bald spot, and I knew there was a chance that if I took too much off there wouldn't be anything left. Another customer who had a full head of hair might say, "Give me a buzz cut." That meant putting the clippers into overdrive, sending them into the "far country," and avoiding cutting one or more of the customer's ears off.

True repentance is all or nothing. It's an *I'm sorry* that runs deep to the soul, deep enough to admit its need and abandon any previous plans for the sake of God's restoration.

Step Three: Confession

"I know my transgressions, and my sin is always before me" (Psalm 51:3).

I heard someone say that confession is simply telling God what He already knows. Why go to the trouble? Simply because it's a step of faith, a second important step in the restoration process (1 John: 1:9).

In my book *Maximum Integrity* I comment on David's trip back from the brink: "He didn't make excuses for his behavior. He did not call his actions mistakes. You may try to deflect guilt by saying 'Everybody makes mistakes.' Two plus two equals five is a mistake. But breaking God's law on purpose isn't a mistake; it's a sin. David acknowledged it."[6]

Step Four: Forgiveness

When we've taken all the other steps, thankfully the last step is Christ's! "He is the one all the prophets testified about, saying that everyone who believes in him will have their sins forgiven through his name" (Acts 10:43, NLT).

Oswald Chambers said, "If Jesus ever commanded us to do something that He was unable to equip us to accomplish, He would be a liar. And if we make our own inability a stumbling block or an excuse not to be obedient, it means that we are telling God that there is something which He has not yet taken into account."[7]

The lessons of his indiscretion.

We all go "to school" on the trips or triumphs of others, just like a golfer watching another golfer putt on the green of a golf course. The path the golfer's golf ball makes toward the cup tells the observing golfer how the greens lie—how the golf ball reacts to the surface.

David's route to failure and back offers some great lessons in living.

No One Is Immune to Sin

David said, "Surely I was sinful at birth, sinful from the time my mother conceived me" (Psalm 51:5). His experience taught him that there was an inherent spiritual gene in the pool. The Bible calls it a carnal nature. Since Adam's first rebellion, everyone is born with a tendency to rebel. "Sin entered the world through one man, and death through sin, and in this way death came to all men, because all sinned" (Romans 5:12).

We Do Not Have to Sin

David was his own snitch: "I know my transgressions, and my sin is always before me" (Psalm 51:3). He wasn't about to blame his spiritual stupidity on his Aunt Edna's penchant for pecadillos, the climate of criticism in the Temple, or the fact that he didn't get to play lead harp in the praise band. *He* was to blame for the Bathsheba chronicles—and he admitted it.

Sin is one person making the choice to pick from Satan's Column B rather than the Savior's Column A—like choosing items on a menu board at a delicatessen.

Paul wrote "What shall we say, then? Shall we go on sinning so that grace may increase? By no means! We died to sin; how can we live in it any longer?" (Romans 6:1).

Whether your parents chose to have you or you're just an inadvertent result of their first anniversary trip to Hawaii, you're still a person of choice. God gave you a free will; you have the right to choose Him or deny Him.

The Only Answer

Create in me a pure heart, O God, and renew a stead-fast spirit within me. Do not cast me from your presence or take your Holy Spirit from me. Restore to me the joy of your salvation and grant me a willing spirit, to sustain me (*Psalm 51:10-12*).

When the solution came, it wasn't about crowns or thrones or servants or temples; it was all about a hungry beggar coming to the giver of life for the *bread of life*.

In the process of solving one relationship problem, he solved two. He discovered that when he improved his relationship with God, his relationships with the others in his social network were vastly improved. Amen.

8

"IN" IS THE DIFFERENCE BETWEEN IN-LAWS AND OUTLAWS

Real Loyalty

Maybe the "in" in "in-law" implies, "If you're in, you're not an outlaw." And then, you might be *in* and still be an "*out*law." It really does vary according to the in-laws and outlaws. As you know, one of the first things that happens to you after you say "I do" is that you gain a nation of relatives to whom you're not a naturally born citizen.

Stephen Arterburn said, "Getting married is our proclamation to the world and to ourselves that we are optimists; it's how we manifest our conviction that not only can we be happy but that we have what it takes to make a whole other person happy."[1]

But the process is often challenging.

George and his new bride, Carla, were adjusting to marriage. Except for the fact that Carla always grabbed the toothpaste and squeezed it in the middle as if she were strangling it, George was learning to accept the quirks of those who've had the same family most of their lives.

Remembering the wedding minister's advice to be honest with one another, George finally got up enough nerve to approach the toothpaste issue. It happened during breakfast.

For George, breakfast had been the same since graduating from college, moving back home, and then moving to an apartment several years later: one egg over medium, not runny; one slice of lightly toasted whole wheat bread; real butter, not margarine; orange juice, not from concentrate and no pulp; and a cup of *naturally* decaffeinated coffee, Maxwell House, his mother's favorite brand.

Carla usually grabbed a protein bar and swigged the last of a Diet Coke.

"Carla," George said seriously, "before you leave for work we need to talk about oral hygiene." That came as a surprise to Carla.

George continued: "It's the toothpaste. Mother taught me to roll the tube up from the bottom. It leaves less residual paste—and it's simply more frugal."

Carla had a reaction just short of a rash and stormed out the door—without a good-bye or a kiss.

That evening George tried to smooth the waters by taking her to his favorite restaurant, Momma's House of Cookin'.

Trying to make conversation on the way, George spotted a mule out in a field and asked humorously, "Is that a relative?"

Carla replied, "It wasn't *before* I married!"

There's an in-law story in the Scriptures that's filled with important principles for bringing out the best in the extended family—in spite of toothpaste-squeezing.

In the days when the judges ruled, there was a famine in the land, and a man from Bethlehem in Judah, together with his wife and two sons, went to live for a while in the country of Moab. The man's name was Elimelech, his wife's name was Naomi, and the names of his two sons were Mahlon and Kilion. They were Ephrathites from Bethlehem, Judah. And they went to Moab and lived there (*Ruth 1:1-2*).

Had the story ended there, it would have been rather Norman Rockwellian. A family facing a crisis had pulled together and made a seemingly uneventful move to a better locale. Certainly it wasn't like calling Two Men and a Truck to haul their stuff to Moab. There were few, if any, Burger Kings along the way, and air conditioning a camel was cost-prohibitive.

But it didn't end there. As in many cases, the best characteristics of an extended family come out in the worst of circumstances.

The interpersonal dynamics provide us with ten principles for successful interfamily relationships.

Value the Gift of Family

Now Elimelech, Naomi's husband, died, and she was left with her two sons. They married Moabite women, one named Orpah and the other Ruth. After they had lived there about ten years, both Mahlon and Kilion also died, and Naomi was left without her two sons and her husband (*Ruth 1:3-5*).

Perhaps Elimelech's death was soon after their arrival in Moab. If so, the death would have added to a family's strain of adjusting to a new home. A world of words is left unspoken in the phrase "and Naomi was left without her two sons and her husband." Though the death of the sons may have been years after arriving in Moab, the cascading circumstances were probably overwhelming.

I can understand.

As noted earlier, in *The Harder I Laugh, the Deeper I Hurt* I describe the events in my childhood after the sudden death of my father. My Uncle Roy picked my brothers and me up from school and drove us to the Doctor's North Hospital in Columbus, Ohio. I remember the aching feeling when a policeman came to the car where we were waiting and informed us that our dad was gone.

My uncle had to help my mother into the house when we returned home. We brothers clung to each other in the car and sobbed until he returned to take us into the house.

It simply didn't make sense. We had moved to Ohio from West Virginia so Dad wouldn't have to work in the coal mines. He suffered from black lung disease and had broken his back three times before he was 30. He had moved our family to Ohio to make life better. Now he was dead! All our hopes for a better life were gone![2]

Just think what those moments would have been like without Uncle Roy being there! And think of the countless times a relative—immediate family or extended family—has stepped in to lend *you* a helping hand.

No wonder the family unit is said to be God-given.

Walter A. Elwell comments in *Baker's Evangelical Dictionary of Biblical Theology,* "In ancient Israel large families were deemed necessary to conduct the family business, to provide for the parents in their old age, and to carry on the family name. As a result, the large family was regarded as a blessing from God [Exodus 1:21; Psalm 128:3]."[3]

He further explains—

Israel's social structure was tribal and therefore corporate (solidary) in its internal relationships, generating tightly structured communities. Whatever their size, these communities perceived themselves as totalities, bound together through internal agencies that made their presence felt in each individual member. The individual was neither overlooked, nor was he considered the unit on which the society was built. Instead, the family was the unit, and the individual found his place in society through the family and its extensions.[4]

Viewing your extended family as a blessing of God rather than a burden of responsibility will help you in your interfamily relationships.

Determine to Work on Family Relationships.

Situations changed once again for Naomi and the survivors. But the changing environment would be an opportunity for the players to reveal their personal best.

When she heard in Moab that the LORD had come to the aid of his people by providing food for them, Naomi and her daughters-in-law prepared to return home from there. With her two daughters-in-law she left the place where she had been living and set out on the road that would take them back to the land of Judah (*Ruth 1:6-7*).

The death of her husband and sons, along with news that times were improving back in Judah, caused Naomi to put Plan B into motion. However, that didn't mean that everyone in the caravan would want to take the interstate rather than the side roads, where all the yard sales were. There would be some concessions along with the repercussions.

- They would have to choose their battles based on the overall good.
- They would have to yield opinion to the wisdom and experience of others.
- They would have to consciously accept the best practices of others.
- They would have to keep still when it would be better to speak out.
- They would have to yield to God's will rather than their own wants.

It's never wise to leap over a ditch in two jumps!

Steady but determined progress would be a matter of personal choice on everyone's part.

I've heard it said that it's never wise to leap over a ditch in two jumps! Keeping an eye on the overall relationship goals gives wisdom to daily actions and reactions.

Use Kind Words as an Expression of Affirmation

Then Naomi said to her two daughters-in-law, "Go back, each of you, to your mother's home. May the LORD show kindness to you, as you have shown to your dead and to me. May the LORD grant that each of you will find rest in the home of another husband." Then she kissed them and they wept aloud and said to her, "We will go back with you to your people" (*Ruth 1:8-10*).

There are times in interfamily relationships when words fail.

I heard of a deer hunter who shot a 300-pound buck. He got to the carcass just as an officer with the Department of Conservation stooped down to admire the 10-point antlers on the huge deer.

"There it is!" the hunter shouted as he broke through a clearing. "Been tracking that thing since five o'clock this morning. Never seen one bigger than that!"

The officer replied, "You're right! That's the largest buck I've seen in this neck of the woods." He took a Craftsmen tape measure off his belt, stretched it out over the carcass, and said casually, "I'm sure you have a deer license?"

The hunter paused to think. "You know, officer, I can't remember if I got one this year or not."

The officer quickly responded, "Well, then, I'm going to have to confiscate this deer for evidence."

With that the conservation officer grabbed the deer antlers and dragged the weighty evidence for nearly a mile to the road.

The hunter followed the exhausted officer all the way back to the main road. Coincidently, the patrol car was parked next to the hunter's jeep.

When they arrived, the hunter suddenly announced, "Thanks, officer. I'll take it from here." He reached into his wallet and pulled out a piece of paper. "I just remembered I have that license."

Talk about your pregnant pause!

Interfamily relationships can be just as frustrating.

- The oldest child decides the home place that has been willed to the surviving children should have chartreuse siding.

- A brother-in-law is running for sheriff in "that other" political party and wants you to nail posters to trees in the community.

- The aged and widowed family patriarch has announced his engagement to a licensed practical nurse from the assisted living facility—who is half his age.

- A sister-in-law has brought a PowerPoint presentation to the family reunion, chronicling her son's three years of band performances. What does he play? A tuba!

In each of those hypothetical situations, a kind word could mean the difference between civility at the next family gathering or a Weather Channel cold front sweeping through the room.

There's always room for a compliment—and in every situation one is buried somewhere in the pile.

- "Chartreuse? My, you certainly have a decorator's eye!"

- "Sheriff? Your independent spirit will make you a fine peace officer."

- "Engaged at eighty-three? Oh, well—at least we'll have a nurse at the family picnic."

- "PowerPoint? I've always wanted to see a tuba up close."

Take a Short-term Loss for the Sake of a Long-term Gain

Naomi took a sacrificial step—a step that would mean immediate uncertainty for her but would provide a more stable environment for her in-laws.

But Naomi said, "Return home, my daughters. Why would you come with me? Am I going to have any more sons, who could become your husbands? Return home, my daughters; I am too old to have another husband (*Ruth 1:11*).

In Bible times, tradition called for the surviving son to marry his brother's widow. In this case, Naomi knew the only acceptable option for her daughters-in-law would be to return to their home country to marry.

Plus, Naomi wasn't about to sign up for one of those online dating services. For two reasons: One, she didn't have cable, and two, she didn't have a computer.

Every Family Member Has Unseen Needs

Pain is present in every family setting, most of it unseen. I have friends, for instance, who may be going through excruciating personal pain but always have a smile. I have other friends who expect a Hallmark card when they get a hangnail. Different strokes for different folks.

Beneath the calm surface, Naomi was struggling emotionally and spiritually.

Even if I thought there was still hope for me—even if I had a husband tonight and then gave birth to sons—would you wait until they grew up? Would you remain unmarried for them? No, my daughters. It is more bitter for me than for you, because the LORD's hand has gone out against me! (*Ruth 1:12-13*).

ﷺ ﷺ ﷺ

**We react to surface needs, forgetting that
everything that surfaces has grown
from the inside out.**

Why does that person act *that* way? The answer is so obvious that often it is overlooked. He or she acts *that* way because of something happening on the inside. We react to surface needs, forgetting that everything that surfaces has been growing from the inside out.

A panicked mother took her two-year-old to the emergency room. After what seemed like several hours of filling out insurance papers, privacy statements, and the second-mortgage papers on their vacation home, mother and daughter were ushered into a treatment room—for another wait.

Just before the two-year-old was ready for kindergarten, a young-looking intern entered the room. "What seems to be our problem?"

The mother replied, "Well I don't know about your problem, but my daughter has swallowed a tiny magnet."

The intern, who looked to be about fourteen, ordered blood work, x-rays, and a CAT scan—most of which sent the two-year-old into a frenzy.

An hour into keeping the little girl still while the tests were read, the intern stepped back into the room. "We saw the magnet. It's there all right. I'd recommend a wait-and-see treatment."

"Wait-and-see?" the mother responded. "Isn't there anything else you can do?"

The intern thought for a while, "Well, I'm new to medicine, so I don't know if this has been done before, but you could try holding her up to the refrigerator door. If she sticks to it, you'll know it's still in there."

A lot of folks—family members included—have swallowed emotional magnets. They've gathered comments and questions and quandaries from long ago. And sometimes you'll be the emergency physician when they have a reaction.

- That burst of anger comes from never being able to please a parent.
- That tear-flooded reaction comes from an abuse they've never made known.
- That protective attitude comes from a childhood plagued with poverty.
- That overconfidence comes from the feelings of worthlessness.

Go ahead and treat the symptoms—in lovingkindness. Soon you'll be the physician-on-call and a best friend when other outbreaks occur. Jesus was—and still is. In Matthew 11:28-29 He said, "Come to me, all you who are weary and burdened, and I will give you rest. Take my yoke upon you and learn from me, for I am gentle and humble in heart, and you will find rest for your souls."

A Unique Personality Changes a Group Dynamic

The in-law saga continues:

At this they wept again. Then Orpah kissed her mother-in-law good-by, but Ruth clung to her. "Look," said Naomi, "your sister-in-law is going back to her people and her gods. Go back with her." But Ruth replied, "Don't urge me to leave you or to turn back from you" (*Ruth 1:14-16*).

Aterburn says, "Whenever any of us get involved in an intense and prolonged group dynamic in which we have a great deal at stake, it can't help but push in us a lot of the same emotional buttons that were installed in us the first time we were ever involved in an intense and prolonged group dynamic."[5]

The daughters-in-law were of a different faith than Naomi. They were raised in a pluralistic culture, worshiping many gods. Naomi was raised to serve Jehovah God. But the differences went beyond faith.

Two daughters-in-law reacted differently, based on their unique personalities. They both shared the same journey, they both openly shared their affection, and they both expressed their emotions.

But something had obviously happened to Ruth. Rather than joining her sister-in-law on the journey back to the old culture, she was drawn to the new. She uniquely expressed her loyalty to her mother-in-law by staying with her. She wasn't a quitter.

So why do some family members cry at funerals while others sit there stoically? Do they not both love the family member? Probably so, but people and personalities are unique. That's what keeps family gatherings so interesting.

It's Thanksgiving. Uncle Fred is on the floor balancing a floor lamp on the soles of his feet while Aunt Martha is reading back issues of *Better Homes & Gardens* in the finished basement family room. Little Edward is stacking the used plastic cups from dinner on the antique desk, trying to make a replica of the Eiffel Tower, while Cousin Monique is doing school cheers on the living room sofa.

Grandpa has missed the whole thing; he's sleeping in the leather recliner as if he's in *Gulliver's Travels*, while Grandma is playing knee-horsey with a newborn 'til the little one throws up.

Is each unique and important to the interfamily relationship?

Have you ever seen a rhesus monkey go around the center ring of a circus, riding on the back of a collie dog? That's my point! Same show, different cast members. Here are some suggestions for handling it:

- Focus on the best of the worst.
- Think of your own peculiarities in light of others.

- Accept family members for who they are and not what they've done.
- Make room for Christ in every judgment.

Commit to the Greater Purpose: Wholeness and Healing

Ruth was the undiscovered gold coin. She might have been tarnished by the times, but beneath the surface she had a greater commitment to a greater cause.

Where you go I will go, and where you stay I will stay. Your people will be my people and your God my God. Where you die I will die, and there I will be buried. May the LORD deal with me, be it ever so severely, if anything but death separates you and me (*Ruth 1:16-17*).

It might have been easier for Ruth to ride double on a camel back to Moab with Orpah. But she had discovered the greater cause: faithfulness to Naomi's God.

No matter the cost, she chose to stay. She found wholeness and healing—enough to free her from the demons of the past and enough to give her a hope for the future.

The cost was minor compared to the consequence: love and marriage with Boaz (see Ruth 3).

Naomi was a puller, not a pusher.

Pull—Don't Push

I like the classic story of the man dragging a huge chain through the yard. Someone walked over to him and asked why he was pulling the chain. Quickly the man held up the chain and responded, "Did you ever try to *push* one of these things?"

Naomi was a puller, not a pusher. "When Naomi realized that Ruth was determined to go with her, she stopped urging her" (Ruth 1:18).

Many interfamily relationships would be smoother if someone traded pushing for pulling. Whether it is a personal, political, philosophical, or preferential agenda, pushing only divides. There are some things that family members just shouldn't discuss when they're together. You know. Right this moment, you can think of dynamite words that will blow the smithereens out of a backyard barbecue with your family.

Paul advised, "Let your conversation be always full of grace, seasoned with salt, so that you may know how to answer everyone" (Colossians 4:6). Don't provide the hot sauce. It's only going to ruin someone's appetite.

Pulling is bringing out the opinions of others—good or bad—for the sake of showing interest in them. Go back through the sent items in your e-mail, if you haven't deleted them, and check how many paragraphs in those e-mails begin with the letter *I*.

If you have *I* problems, you'll certainly have interrelationship problems. Back to the words of an old Sunday School song: "Jesus and others and you—that's a wonderful way to spell JOY."

Let Your Life Do the Talking

So the two women went on until they came to Bethlehem. When they arrived in Bethlehem, the whole town was stirred because of them, and the women exclaimed, "Can this be Naomi?" (*Ruth 1:19*).

John Wesley noted, "Is this she that formerly lived in so much plenty and honour? How marvelously is her condition changed!"[6]

Maybe the next verse explains it:

"Don't call me Naomi," she told them. "Call me Mara because the Almighty has made my life very bitter. I went away full, but the LORD has brought me back empty. Why call me Naomi? The LORD has afflicted me; the Almighty has brought misfortune upon me" (*Ruth 1:20-21*).

She would certainly be the subject of the ladies' Tuesday morning Bible study. "Girl, did you see how that Naomi looked when she got back from Moab?"

"Did I see her! She looked like she'd been run over by a chariot pulling a disc plow!"

"Her hair looked as if she hadn't been to the beauty parlor since Eve got her that new fall wardrobe!"

But there's one in every crowd—one who will break through the ice and see the sunshine. "Granted, she really looked different. She didn't have all that pomp and glory she used to have—there was something even richer about her."

It catches on. "Yeah, there was a character, a maturity about her that she didn't have before she left."

"And that daughter-in-law—what's her name? Oh, yes—Naomi. She had that same religious look. But don't misunderstand me. It looked sincere—really sincere."

Naomi had turned her past into new beginnings. "So Naomi returned from Moab accompanied by Ruth the Moabitess, her daughter-in-law, arriving in Bethlehem as the barley harvest was beginning" (Ruth 1:22).

She let her life do the talking, just as Jesus instructed everyone in every situation—even interfamily situations: "You are the light of the world—like a city on a mountain, glowing in the night for all to see. Don't hide your light under a basket! Instead, put it on a stand and let it shine for all. In the same way, let your good deeds shine out for all to see, so that everyone will praise your heavenly Father" (Matthew 5:14-16, NLT).

9

IF THEY DIDN'T LEAVE THE LIGHT ON, IT MUST BE THE INN
Real Love

Wayne Cordeiro writes of a father who was in such a hurry for his son to get through college that he even asked its president, James A. Garfield, who later became a United States president, to intervene. "Is there any way you can get my son through this institution faster than four years?" He implored. "Time is running short, and the business world is waiting!"

"It all depends on what you want," Garfield wisely replied. "Squash will take only three months, but if you want oak, that requires four years."[1]

Twenty-first-century love also seems to be the victim of a hectic lifestyle, with couples expressing lifelong commitments to people they've known only short-term via the Internet. And "real love" is often expressed in a one-year lease on an apartment by folks who may call themselves "engaged" for a decade but are as uncertain about their future as a snowflake in the Sahara.

Real love has its legends, folks who have exemplified its highest ideals. For example, we watched the televised memorial service for Ruth Bell Graham, when her husband of sixty-plus years, Billy Graham, feebly stood to his feet, clutched a microphone in his Parkinson's-affected hand, and spoke so tenderly of his wife. It wasn't in the booming voice of the evangelist who had spoken to over two hundred million people. It was in a soft, ailing voice that called her an "incredible woman."

He looked toward the pine casket, constructed by prisoners to whom she had ministered, and said he spent hours looking at her in her casket and praying, and wished that everyone could see how beautiful she looked.

Ruth Graham had been the less profiled of the famous family, choosing to stay home in their North Carolina mountain home and raise their children while Dr. Graham preached around the globe. But to those who knew her or read her books or felt her prayers, she wasn't any less esteemed.

The New Testament chronicles a beautiful love story as well, between Mary and Joseph. Next to the Christ child, the main character has always been the wife, Mary. Her husband, Joseph, was of a lower profile, but his tender faithfulness modeled everything the apostle Paul said about earthly love in often quoted 1 Corinthians 13:

Love is patient, love is kind. It does not envy, it does not boast, it is not proud. It is not rude, it is not self-seeking, it is not easily angered, it keeps no record of wrongs. Love does not delight in evil but rejoices with the truth. It always protects, always trusts, always hopes, always perseveres (*1 Corinthians 13:4-7*).

A friend of mine said he saw a church's online newsletter "casting call" for its Christmas production. It listed the characters and described each one's role, or persona. Some would have inspiring solo parts, others would be in the chorus, and others would be the bad guys—all speaking parts. When it came to casting Joseph, the announcement said, "This is a non-speaking part."

That's pretty much the way it's been since the real event at Bethlehem. But I think Joseph spoke as much or more by his actions than he could have by his words—modeling the best practices of Paul's principles. See how the principles of 1 Corinthians 13 blend with the Gospels' account of Joseph and Mary (see Matthew 1—2 and Luke 2).

Love Is Patient; Love Is Kind

This is how the birth of Jesus Christ came about: His mother Mary was pledged to be married to Joseph, but before they came together, she was found to be with child through the Holy Spirit. Because Joseph her husband was a righteous man and did not want to expose her to public disgrace, he had in mind to divorce her quietly (*Matthew 1:18-19*).

You would have to open the books of Jewish history to see the real dynamics of this relationship; how nearly everything that transpired at the beginning was so contradictory to the definitions of their society. Yet Joseph was willing to go the distance for the young woman he loved.

Joseph loved Mary in spite of the uncertainty of her condition. "She was found to be with child through the Holy Spirit" (Matthew 1:18).

Real love doesn't have to have all the puzzle pieces in place to see the greater picture.

Real love doesn't have to have all the puzzle pieces in place to see the greater picture. Joseph and Mary had been planning for a wedding, but the plans took a detour.

Allow me. Perhaps the caterer had been picked out and the fellowship center next to the Temple scheduled. Perhaps, as is often the case, the soloist hadn't yet rehearsed "You Are the Wind Beneath My Wings," when suddenly all the wind was taken out of their wings.

Can you imagine that talk? Joseph may have started the conversation, "Mary, my love, you look tired. Are you sure you're getting enough rest?"

Mary might have said, "I'm fine, Joseph. But now that you mention it, I haven't had a lot of sleep lately. I don't know whether I told you this, but an angel from heaven said I would be having a child—God's child."

Joseph might have had a lump in his throat the size of cruise ship towing a row boat.

"Having a child? God's child?" You don't know whether you *told me?*"

Eyewitness News didn't have "team coverage" on the scene, but based on the circumstances, I think he was probably a little tense. I also think he didn't make a tsunami out of the surprise.

Of course, he had to process it. This was a hundred miles out of his comfort zone. But in the end, God's plan would be Joseph's *command.*

The love expressed by the virgin girl who became the earthly mother of the heavenly Savior is the centerpiece of the wonderful story. Yet we just can't leave out the integral part Joseph played in the entire scenario. His actions and reactions were noble and righteous and gracious.

In fact, every husband and wife could learn about relationships from Joseph's behavior. Life happens. Much of it is unscripted. It would be nice if we could plan out the setting, the characters, the stage, and the drama. But it's more like an improvisation. We make up the script as we go.

- The characters often appear without warning on the stage —some good guys, some bad.
- The stage is usually in the round. There are no defining edges.

- The drama—though "directed" by our Heavenly Father—unfolds spontaneously.

Yet patience, love, and kindness will make a difference in a hit or a flop. The audience will go away with either a warm feeling or an angry resentment. It's up to you and me—and the grace of Christ working through us.

I like the story of the Vacation Bible School teacher who had just talked about the prodigal son and his welcome back home. She added "One person in the story didn't rejoice. Can anyone tell me who this was?"

A hand was raised from the second row of folding chairs. "I know!"

"Who was it?" the teacher asked.

The little voice said, "Was it the fatted calf?"[2]

Joseph might have felt a little bit like the fatted calf in the celebration. He was there, but not every part of the festivities was that enjoyable.

Joseph loved Mary in spite of the cost to his belief. "Joseph . . . was a righteous man" (Matthew 1:19). This whole thing was so off the charts for a man whose Sabbath was spent in the synagogue, whose reading list always included the Decalogue, and whose daily prayers came from the core of a devout heart. Even if the phrase had been invented, "single parent" wouldn't have been a part of his daily vocabulary. But his love for God and for his fiancé kept him in the competition.

Here's the question: Is relationship a priority over religion? The answer is no. God said there would be no other gods before Him. His Son would say, "Seek first His kingdom and His righteousness." Faith and family would have to blend. Allowance for one would not offset the other, but first things first if there is to be a happy relationship (see Matthew 6:33).

In fact, the one would nurture the other. A faith triangle is clearly seen. It's a tried-and-true principle: the closer two people grow in faith and relationship, the closer they move toward God.

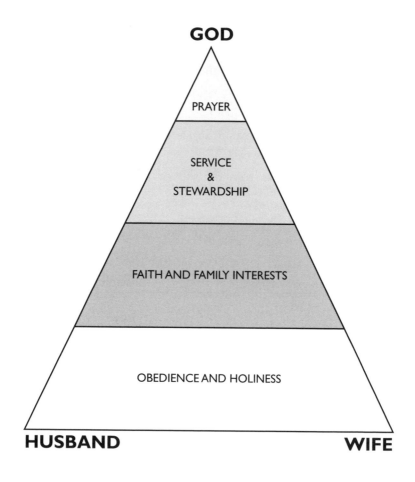

Joseph loved Mary in spite of the opinions of others. "Joseph . . . did not want to expose her to public disgrace" (Matthew 1:19). Joseph would be "perspiringly" uncomfortable at the next men's group breakfast. His fiancé was sewing booties while he hadn't even been sewing his oats!

In Bible times engagement was more than a diamond ring bought at Target—it was a serious and lifelong commitment—

treated as if it were a real marriage. To the audience, it seemed that Mary had broken her vows to Joseph.

**Joseph's calling was more important
than the critiques of the crowd.**

But Joseph's calling was more important than the critiques of the crowd. He would reach out to Mary, loving her, cherishing her in spite of her circumstances.

Love Does Not Envy, Does Not Boast, and Is Not Proud

That doesn't say Joseph didn't have his anxious moments. Again, allow me. Joseph wasn't your GQ kind of guy. He probably wasn't voted most likely to succeed during his high school days—or president of the student council in college. But his outdoor job would have given him a handsome edge. Probably he was muscled from his work as a carpenter and naturally tanned from being in the sun—not one of those rented tans from the tanning salon.

His broadband service might have been basic, since his tweets or texts probably wouldn't overload the circuits of his Internet service provider. His family lineage would have given him a high social ranking—had it been made known. But his love for Mary broke the barriers. He was willing to put his pride on a spiritual shelf and not take it down.

At first, the news was a bit more than he could handle; but he reconciled it out of his love for Mary.

But after he had considered this, an angel of the Lord appeared to him in a dream and said, "Joseph son of David, do not be afraid to take Mary home as your wife, because what is conceived in her is from the Holy Spirit. She will give birth to a son, and you are to give him the name Jesus, because he will save his people from their sins" (*Matthew 1:20-21*).

She would give birth to a *son*, the patriarchal plum in Eastern culture. Now if only the maternity circumstances were under his control. He felt as helpless as a polar bear on a melting ice flow. In a best-case situation, the birth would have been celebrated. In this case, he wasn't so sure. The son would be scorned because He would be born "out of wedlock."

When one person insists on being the center of attention, that pretty much limits the coverage of the rest of the limelight!

But Joseph would not scorn Him or abandon Him—or ridicule His mother. Prideful boasting had no place in this situation.

Selfish pride often becomes the glitch in relationships. When one person insists on being the center of attention, that pretty much limits the coverage of the rest of the limelight!

Author and seminary president Wayne Schmidt wrote,

The mind is not disconnected from the spirit. Many a closed mind can be directly traced to an unteachable spirit. An unteachable spirit is not a "mental" problem but the evidence of an inward arrogance and carnal pride that imagines one's superiority to others. Only genuine repentance can remedy this sinful malady and clear the way for renewing of the mind.[3]

I heard of a new driver whose father took him out on the interstate to test his driving skills. There were four lanes each way, all filled with traffic. The boy looked as tense as a cucumber at a tossed salad competition. He grabbed the wheel and *aimed*.

Soon the father was as tense as the son. The new driver was going seventy miles an hour in the slow lane—and edging right. "Watch out—you're too close to the shoulder!" The father shouted. "And you just missed our exit!"

The son replied in the same tone of voice, "How else can I do a U-turn?"

Joseph didn't panic. There wasn't a U-turn in his future; he was going in God's direction.

Joseph didn't envy Mary's favor or the child's adoration. What if you were in a relationship with someone and having dinner with him or her at Applebee's when all of a sudden an angel announces over the loud speaker that your soul mate was "highly favored" and asks for the employees and customers to applaud? How would that make you feel?

Mary's favor was a zillion times more recognized. Prophets saw the birth announcements thousands of years before Bethlehem. Her cousin's unborn child did a cartwheel in the womb when she walked by. Angels rehearsed a gala in the heavens before the announcement of her child's birth emblazoned the skies of Judah.

"And what are your plans, Joseph?"

"Uh—well—I plan to continue my carpentry business and take care of my wife and family."

Had he been a regular Bubba, he would have gone into a super-sized slump; but he wasn't your regular Bubba—he was a man with a heavenly mission. Come to think of it, anyone with a heavenly mission is not your "regular" person. The Bible calls Joseph a righteous man—a man of marble character (see Matthew 1:19).

I simply think it's important to see how godly character was molded in the very human lives of Joseph and Mary.

Joseph was willing to play second coronet in the orchestra. He knew from the moment of the surprise announcement that Mary would be playing lead violin. And the baby would be the guest soloist. But the *cause* was greater than the *applause.*

I don't mean to trivialize the blessedness of the announcement or the sacredness of any part of this relationship. I simply think it's important to see how godly character was molded in the very human lives of Joseph and Mary. A young man and an innocent teenage lady were about to nurture, feed, and clothe God himself. How could any of us truly understand the enormity of their task?

Joseph's reaction wasn't one of arrogance but rather of servanthood. It's a lesson for all of us servants. If you want to bring out the best in your relationship, bring out the best in your partner. Let your partner know that you understand his or her worth—then acknowledge it in word and deed.

Joseph didn't boast of his heritage. Joseph was a strong twig on the branch of the family tree. He was a descendant of David. He could have played the "lineage" card at any time, but he chose rather to play the devoted husband and father card.

Mary was a commoner of sorts. Her family wasn't well-known. Though her family tree had roots that intertwined through the tribe of Judah all the way back to the throne of David as well, she was young and relatively unknown in her hometown of Nazareth.

All that changed with a word from the angel Gabriel.

The angel went to her and said, "Greetings, you who are highly favored! The Lord is with you." Mary was greatly troubled at his words and wondered what kind of greeting this might be. But the angel said to her, "Do not be afraid, Mary, you have found favor with God. You will be with child and give birth to a son, and you are to give him the name Jesus" (*Luke 1:28-31*).

There are many lessons in this wonderful story, but one that should be mentioned here is this: we should never underestimate the contribution of one person to a relationship. A carpenter, a commoner, and a Christ were inextricably linked together in an historical and redemptive bond. Opposites may not only attract—they may also bring significant and unique skills to a relationship. That is a cause for celebration, not resentment.

Love Is Neither Rude nor Self-Seeking

All this took place to fulfill what the Lord had said through the prophet: "The virgin will be with child and will give birth to a son, and they will call him Immanuel"—which means, "God with us." When Joseph woke up, he did what the angel of the Lord had commanded him and took Mary home as his wife. But he had no union with her until she gave birth to a son. And he gave him the name Jesus (*Matthew 1:22-25*).

Joseph didn't put his own needs first. His marriage celebration wasn't exactly the one Joseph had in mind growing up in Nazareth. News of Mary's condition probably made it around town faster than a donkey with its tail on fire. Joseph must have been aware of the talk: "Did you hear about Mary and that poor Joseph?" He might not have gotten respect from the townsfolk, but he deserved some recognition at home, as a husband. After all, he had human needs just like everyone else, and Mary was his covenant bride.

Love isn't rude. It doesn't value its needs above the needs of another.

Love isn't rude. It doesn't value its needs above the needs of another. Joseph wasn't taking his cues from some Dr. Phil type; he was taking cues from heaven. *He did what the Lord had commanded him.* The "rights" he had as a marriage partner were not greater than the needs of his wife. I think his attitude could have a significant impact on marital relationships.

Focus on the Family writers Greg Johnson and Mike Yorkey quoted James Dobson's warning about wrong motives in marital sex.

- It is often permitted as a marital duty.
- It is offered to repay or secure a favor.
- It represents conquest or victory.
- It stands as a substitute for verbal communication.
- It is used to overcome feelings of inferiority—especially by men who seek proof of their masculinity.
- It is an enticement for emotional love—especially by women who use their bodies to obtain masculine attention.
- It is a defense against anxiety and tension.
- It is provided or withheld in order to manipulate the partner.
- It is engaged in for the purpose of bragging to others.

Johnson and Yorkey add, "Recognizing them (with yourself), admitting them (to your wife), and making honest attempts at solving selfish motives (with God's help) will foster a level of trust that marriages need for long-term health."[4]

Joseph delighted to obey the word of the Lord. From the trip to Egypt to the naming of the child, Joseph's delight was in pleasing God. It is interesting how one person's God-pleasing aids in pleasing others!

I recall a heartwarming story of famed evangelist Dwight L. Moody. Moody was sitting on the platform during the introductory music in one of his crusades when he spotted someone in the audience with whom he had a well-publicized disagreement. In front of the huge crowd, Mr. Moody walked off the platform toward the man as the man walked toward him at the same time. They met in the center aisle. Moody hadn't said a word before the audience member reached out his hand and said, "Mr. Moody, I forgive you."[5]

The gesture was electric. One step of obedience in obeying God's cue brought spiritual anointing to the entire service. What's your step? What words or actions could be healed by a single gesture of obedience to God?

Love Is Not Easily Angered and Keeps No Record of Wrongs

Nothing about Joseph's family life was convenient. He had hardly had time to burn the wrapping paper from the wedding presents before he was given another assignment.

An angel of the Lord appeared to Joseph in a dream. "Get up," he said, "take the child and his mother and escape to Egypt. Stay there until I tell you, for Herod is going to search for the child to kill him." So he got up, took the child and his mother during the night and left for Egypt, where he stayed until the death of Herod. And so was fulfilled what the Lord had said through the prophet: "Out of Egypt I called my son" (*Matthew 2:13-15*).

Actor Jim Carrey said, "Behind every great man is a woman rolling her eyes."[6] The hidden sandbars in a relationship often make for rough sailing. The unexpressed unhappiness, the closeted resentments, the buried doubts—Joseph could have been a poster child for Complainers Anonymous. After all, he was the point man for the name-calling, the sudden travel plans, and the last-minute accommodations, yet he wasn't privy to the greatest announcement of all time.

Of course, it wasn't easy for Mary either, by any means. She bore the life-changing secret. She endured the difficult pregnancy conditions, and she gave birth in a manger cave.

Joseph didn't express anger for his circumstances. Everything I read about Joseph brings me to the same conclusion: Joseph was a gentle man of great character and compassion. The *New Evangelical Translation* of the Bible comments, "If a type is to be sought in the character of Joseph, it is that of a simple, honest, hardworking, God-fearing man, who was possessed of large sympathies and a warm heart. Strict in the observance of Jewish law and custom, he was yet ready when occasion arose to make these subservient to the greater law of the Spirit."[7]

Joseph was a gentle man of great character and compassion.

Leo Tolstoy said, "All happy families resemble one another, but each unhappy family is unhappy in its own way." Like a crack in the ceiling of a home eventually becomes the "great divide," breaks in the surface of a relationship grow wider—and usually come from one source.

I heard of a husband who knew the honeymoon was over when he tried to replace the fluorescent light fixture in the garage. Just as he was about to remove the fixture, the ladder slipped. The fixture flew one way, the bulb flew another, and Mr. Fix-it took flight like an eagle that had spotted a rabbit in a cornfield—downward, fast and furious.

His bride of 36 months heard the commotion and ran to the garage. Luckily for the fluorescent fixture repairman, she was a trauma room nurse at a local hospital.

She immediately went over to the fallen do-it-yourselfer, who was lying on the garage floor in the circle of sawdust that covered the remnants of an oil leak.

In a voice of someone who just reported a shooting to the 911 operator, she yelled, "Kevin! Are those your new Dockers?"

Nowhere in Scripture is Mary seen as anything but a loving, reverent, and dutiful servant of God. Had she seen Joseph fall off a ladder and responded like the trauma nurse wife, it might have been Joseph's "last straw." But as we've seen, Joseph probably wouldn't have reacted with anger.

A Chinese proverb says, "If you are patient in one moment of anger, you will escape a hundred days of sorrow." If you look over your relationships—family or otherwise—you'll probably remember an angry reaction that resulted in a "chain reaction." Anger is a malady more contagious than swine flu. During the H1N1 crisis of 2009-2010 there were signs everywhere that read "Cover your cough." And people were actually photographed kissing through flu masks.

I guess I would have to say that if you want to immediately improve a relationship, cover your mouth. In other words, when you're tempted to react angrily, just *don't*.

Joseph didn't keep a record of his sacrifices. My brother Mark tells of a Sunday School teacher who was reviewing the lessons on the Ten Commandments with his third-grade class. "What's the commandment that refers to fathers and mothers?"

"Honor thy father and thy mother," a boy on the front row answered.

"Can you think of another commandment that's important to the family?" he asked. "How about a commandment for brothers and sisters?"

"I know!" a little girl yelled from the back row. "Thou shalt not kill!"[8]

Living with one mother and a house full of brothers, Terry, Mark, and I have stories of how we were seemingly wronged by another brother. And Mark could probably tell you how Terry and I had him try to break the world's record for holding his breath! Looking back, none of us count any of that activity as a "wrong."

In legalese, you might say that Joseph didn't keep the "rights" to his wrongs. Paul said, "Love doesn't keep a record."

Love Does Not Delight in Evil but Rejoices in Truth

After Herod died, an angel of the Lord appeared in a dream to Joseph in Egypt and said, "Get up, take the child and his mother and go to the land of Israel, for those who were trying to take the child's life are dead." So he got up, took the child and his mother and went to the land of Israel. But when he heard that Archelaus was reigning in Judea in place of his father Herod, he was afraid to go there. Having been warned in a dream, he withdrew to the district of Galilee, and he went and lived in a town called Nazareth. So was fulfilled what was said through the prophets: "He will be called a Nazarene" (*Matthew 2:19-23*).

Joseph delighted in the promise of God. He trusted God with the uncertainties of the future, because God said He would take care of them—and God doesn't lie. "Trust God from the bottom of your heart; don't try to figure out everything on your own. Listen for God's voice in everything you do, everywhere you go; he's the one who will keep you on track" (Proverbs 3:5-5, TM).

Can God be trusted with your uncertainties? Compare the promises of Isaiah 7—9 with the kept promises in the Nativity story of the Gospels: persons and events (Isaiah 7:14), environment and announcement (Isaiah 9:2), fulfillment of redemption (Isaiah 9:6). Even the town of birth was promised: "But you, Bethlehem Ephrathah, though you are small among the clans of Judah, out of you will come for me one who will be ruler over Israel, whose origins are from of old, from ancient times" (Micah 5:2).

Joseph delighted in the provisions of God. Maybe there wasn't a first floor, poolside, no-smoking area, or handicapped access in the main building of the inn where Mary could give birth to the Christ child, but heaven's "room reservations" were still honored.

God's answers often don't have same-day delivery like products from the shopping channel. But they come in His way and in His time, every day, moment-by-moment, always on time. We even sing about them:

> *Morning by morning new mercies I see.*
> *All I have needed Thy hand hath provided.*
> *Great is Thy faithfulness, Lord, unto me!*
> —Thomas O. Chisholm

Love Protects, Trusts, Hopes, and Perseveres

So Joseph also went up from the town of Nazareth in Galilee to Judea, to Bethlehem the town of David, because he belonged to the house and line of David. He went there to register with Mary, who was pledged to be married to him and was expecting a child. While they were there, the time came for the baby to be born, and she gave birth to her firstborn, a son. She wrapped him in cloths and placed him in a manger, because there was no room for them in the inn (*Luke 2:1-7*).

• Joseph provided the best he knew how, in God's strength.
• Joseph provided the leadership Mary needed most, in God's wisdom.
• Joseph provided the character traits that Jesus modeled on earth as God's representative.

David L. Thompson wrote, "Families are not simply a collection of individuals, unaffected by other members in the family, capable of being isolated from the others and treated as though their problems or promises were singularly their own. Families live and die together. The attitudes, behavior, health, or lack of it of any member, particularly of its primary caregivers, affect the well-being of all other members."[9]

CONCLUSION
Ten Rules for Relationships

🐟 Anybody who thinks he or she has have trouble sorting out relationships should hear the story of seventy-six-year-old Bill Baker, who wed Edna Harvey in London. Edna was Bill's granddaughter's husband's mother, which was the source of the trouble, according to Baker's granddaughter, Lynn. She explained: "My mother-in-law is now my step-grandmother. My grandfather is now my stepfather-in-law. My mom is my sister-in-law, and my brother is my nephew. But even crazier is that I'm now married to my uncle, and my own children are my cousins."[1]

It can be hard work to sort out relationships. After considering subjects such as conflict, restoration, and forgiveness, you might be wondering, *Who needs relationships anyway?*

You do! God made us to be social beings. We really do need each other.

According to Bernie Siegel, single men are jailed more often, earn less, suffer more illnesses, and die younger than married men. And married men with cancer live twenty percent longer than single men with the same cancer. Also, women, who often have more close friendships than men, survive longer with the same cancers.[2]

Being a friend—or a brother, mother, or in-law, for that matter—is hard work, but it's worth it. Our relationships are like the air we breathe. Both are keeping us alive!

My hope is that you will apply the life lessons I've shared in this book and that you will feel genuine joy in your relationships with those around you. To do that, you will need to master the art of relating to others in each of the five relational contexts:

- **Lifestyle**—work, school, church, or community
- **Family**—immediate and extended family relationships
- **Support**—lay or professional services
- **Development**—career contacts, referral networks
- **Online**—social media networks

The Toler Ten

Whether it's with your boss at work, your Facebook friends, or your in-laws from Poughkeepsie, you need strong, healthy relationships in order to be a strong, healthy person. Here are the Toler Ten, simple rules for relationships that will help you begin to apply the principles in this book.

1. Always say hello. When it comes to greeting others, some behave as if they're taking out the trash—waiting for someone else to do it first. Always be the first one to say hello. Acknowledging another person's presence, whether it's your spouse, your coworker, or a total stranger, is a great way to get a relationship off on the right foot.

2. Smile! Did you know that it takes seventy-two muscles to form a frown but only fourteen to smile? A friendly smile will warm up any room and can even break the ice between people in conflict. Let your face say, "I like you," and you'll receive much goodwill in return. Try this experiment: smile at every person you encounter for one day, and see how many smile in return. I'm guessing it will be one hundred percent!

3. Be generous. Two men were out hunting in the northern United States. Suddenly, one yelled, and the other looked up to see a grizzly charging them. The first started to frantically put on his tennis shoes, and his friend anxiously asked, "What are you doing? Don't you know you can't outrun a grizzly bear?"

"I don't have to outrun a grizzly," the first man replied. "I just have to outrun you!"

Sometimes it seems as if life is a competition, and the only way to succeed is to get ahead of others. In fact, the opposite is true. We get along better when we work together.

Decide to be a giver. Be willing to help out, lend a hand, run an errand, or make a contribution. That goes for your time, your talent, and your treasure. Always give to others more than you take. Bless others, and you'll be blessed yourself.

4. Remember names. Everyone loves to hear the sound of his or her own name. Using a person's name says, "You matter to me." Make an effort to remember names, and use them frequently.

5. Forget mistakes. Nothing is friendlier than a wet dog, and it seems that people who need relationships are the most uncomfortable to be around—just like a wet dog. Make the decision that you will not hold others' faults against them. Forget about the time your sister forgot your birthday or your boss raised his or her voice. Accept the fact that the people around you are less than perfect. Don't make little problems into big ones, and you'll have few big problems.

6. Be the first to apologize. Pride is poison to a relationship; forgiveness is a healing balm. You can untangle many of the problems in relationships with these simple words: *I'm sorry.* "I'm sorry I forgot to call you." "I think my e-mail got us off on the wrong foot—I'm sorry." "I'm sorry we've been out of touch lately." If you begin to thaw the ice, it will soon melt away.

7. Listen more than you talk. The lines of communication in a relationship are like fishing line—both get snarled quite easily. The best way to untangle them is to close your mouth and open your ears. Listen to hear the *heart* of the other person, not just the words. Try to understand both those you like and those you don't, and you'll find that you have plenty of friends and few enemies.

8. *Be respectful.* Maybe it's my West Virginia upbringing, but I still love to hear the words *Sir, Ma'am, please,* and *thank you.* I think everyone does. We all respond better to those who treat us with respect. Whether you are correcting your own children or arguing a point with your boss, be sure to accord others the same dignity that you would like to receive. The Golden Rule still works.

9. *Laugh, laugh, laugh!* It's been estimated by researchers at the University of Michigan that the average child laughs 150 times a day but the average adult laughs only 15 times.[3] No wonder children get along better than adults! Develop the habit of finding humor in every situation, and you'll find less tension and greater harmony in your relationships. Don't take life too seriously. Remember a good line and share it with a friend. Be willing to poke a little fun at yourself. Find the lighter side of your situation, and every problem will be easier to solve.

10. *Remove the plank from your own eye.* Jesus said in Matthew 7:3-5 that before we attempt to remove a speck of sawdust from someone else's eye, we should remove the plank from our own eye first. That was a not-so-subtle way of telling us that we should examine ourselves before being critical of others. Many of our relationship issues could be solved by applying that simple advice. Take an honest look at how you're relating to people. What problems do you discover—on your side? Correct these first. Then you'll be in a great position to work on your relationships with others.

You Can!

Sometimes it seems difficult to get a handle on forming good relationships. Comedian Rodney Dangerfield used to say that he told his father, "Nobody likes me," to which his father replied, "Don't say that—not everybody has met you yet!" If you've ever felt that way, I encourage you to keep working at being a friend. As a child of God, created in His image, you have a lot to offer. The world needs your gifts, your personality, your sense of humor, and your compassion.

So go ahead—begin working on the relationships in your life. You are loved, and we need you!

NOTES

Chapter 1

1. Mary Lou Retton, *Mary Lou Retton's Gateways to Happiness* (Colorado Springs: Waterbrook Press, 2000), 70.

2. Bryan Dean, "WW II Veterans Reunite for First Time Since War," *The Oklahoman*, September 12, 2009, 12A.

3. Stan Toler, *I Love God's Sense of Humor; I Just Wish He'd Let Me In on the Joke* (Kansas City: Beacon Hill Press of Kansas City, 2006), 137.

4. Stephen Covey, <http://www.quoteland.com/topic.asp?CATEGORY_ID=200>.

5. Tony Dungy, *Quiet Strength: The Principles, Practices, and Priorities of a Winning Life* (Carol Stream, Ill.: Tyndale House Publishers, 2007), 105.

6. Anita Renfroe, quoted by Andy Simmons in "Mirth Mother," *Reader's Digest*, September 2009, 116.

Chapter 2

1. Alan Loy McGinnis, *The Friendship Factor* (Minneapolis: Augsburg Publishing House, 1979), 24.

2. Tara Parker-Pope, "What Are Friends For? A Longer Life," *New York Times*, April 20, 2009, <http://www.nytimes.com/2009/04/21/health/21well.html?_r=2&em>.

3. News release, May 30, 2005, Group Publishing, <http://www.childrensministry.com/magazine/extras/2005/NewReleaseandFactSheet.pdf>.

4. Les and Leslie Parrot, *Relationships* (Grand Rapids: Zondervan Publishing House, 1998), 75.

5. <http://www.brainyquote.com/quotes/authors/w/walter_winchell.html>.

6. Ibid.

7. <http://www.brainyquote.com/quotes/keywords/kind.html>.

8. Jamieson, Faussett, and Brown, <http://www.ewordtoday.com/comments/1samuel/jfb/1samuel18.htm>.

9. Stan Toler, *The Inspirational Speaker's Resource* (Kansas City: Beacon Hill Press of Kansas City, 2009), 128.

10. Stan Toler, *ReThink Your Life* (Indianapolis: Wesleyan Publishing House, 2008), 118.

11. Ralph Waldo Emerson, quoted in Elizabeth Dole, *Hearts Touched by Fire: My 500 Favorite Quotations* (New York: Caroll & Graf Publishers, 2004), 83.

12. <http://www.allthingsworkplace.com/2007/12/index.html>.

13. <http://www.rbc.org/devotionals/my-utmost-for-his-highest/01/07/devotion.aspx?year=2009>.

14. Sharon Jaynes, *Celebrating a Christ-Centered Christmas* (Chicago: Moody Publishers, 2001), n.p.

Chapter 3

1. Gerald Ford, quoted in *Hearts Touched by Fire*, 121.

2. Lillian Glass, *Attracting Terrific People* (New York: St. Martin's Press, 1997), 73.

3. <http://www.twainquotes.com/Humor.html>.

4. Francis Shaeffer, "Mere Christianity" (full attribution details unknown).

5. <http://forgivenessfoundation.org/quotes.htm>.

6. Stan Toler, *God Is Never Late; He's Never Early; He's Always Right On Time* (Kansas City: Beacon Hill Press of Kansas City, 2004), 119-20.

Chapter 4

1. <http://www.localhistories.org/oldtestament.html>.

2. Toler, *The Inspirational Speaker's Resource*, 56-57.

3. Stan Toler and Debra White Smith, *The Harder I Laugh, the Deeper I Hurt* (Kansas City: Beacon Hill Press of Kansas City, 2001), 24-27.

4. Bonnie Barrows Thomas, *Wings of Joy*, ed. Joan Winmill Brown (Old Tappan, N.J.: Fleming H. Revell Company, 1997), 34.

5. Hyrum W. Smith, *What Matters Most: The Power of Living Your Values* (New York: Simon & Schuster, 200), 210.

Chapter 5

1. MSNBC News, September 30, 2009, <http://www.msnbc.msn.com/id/33088053/ns/us_news-weird_news/>.

2. Tal D. Bonham, *The Treasury of Clean Jokes* (Nashville: Broadman Press, 1981), 59.

3. George Barna, "New Marriage and Divorce Statistics Released," <http://www.barna.org/barna-update/article/15-familykids/42-new-marriage-and-divorce-statistics-released>.

4. Ibid.

5. <http://dictionary.reference.com/browse/neglect>.

6. David J. Lieberman, *Make Peace with Anyone* (New York: St. Martin's Press, 2002), 22-23.